Business Ethics
and the Law

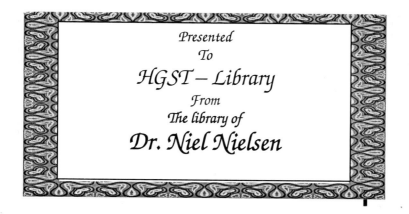

Presented
To
HGST – Library
From
The library of
Dr. Niel Nielsen

D1736401

The Rockwell Lecture Series

Niels Nielsen and Werner Kelber
General Editors

Vol. 2

PETER LANG
New York · San Francisco · Bern
Frankfurt am Main · Paris · London

William W. May

Business Ethics
and the Law

Beyond Compliance

Rockwell Lecture Series
February 1989
Rice University

PETER LANG
New York · San Francisco · Bern
Frankfurt am Main · Paris · London

1741.4
May

25084

12.00

Library of Congress Cataloging-in-Publication Data

May, William W.
    Business ethics and the law : beyond compliance /
William W. May.
    p. cm. — (The Rockwell lecture series : vol. 2)
    Includes bibliographical references.
    1. Business enterprises—United States—Moral and
ethical aspects.   2. Trade regulation—United States.
3. Business ethics—United States.   4. Industry—Social
aspects—United States.   I. Title.   II. Series.
KF1355.M25   1991   174.4'0973—dc20   91-23017
ISBN 0-8204-1728-9   CIP
ISSN 0-1052-2204

Die Deutsche Bibliothek-CIP-Einheitsaufnahme

May, William W.:
Business ethics and the law : beyond compliance / William
W. May.—New York; Berlin; Bern; Frankfurt/M.; Paris;
Wien: Lang, 1991
    (The Rockwell Lecture series ; Vol. 2)
    ISBN 0-8204-1728-9
NE: Rockwell Lecture: The Rockwell Lecture. . .

The paper in this book meets the guidelines for permanence and durability of
the Committee on Production Guidelines for Book Longevity of the
Council on Library Resources.

© Peter Lang Publishing, Inc., New York 1991

Printed in the United States of America.

Contents

Preface vii

Lecture 1
The Limits of Loyalty: A Question of Disclosure   1

Lecture 2
When Rights Collide: The Dial-a-Porn Puzzle 37

Lecture 3
The Meaning of Integrity:
The Use of Proprietary Information 79

Preface

An essential ethical question for business firms is what, if anything, is required beyond what the law prohibits or requires. In these lectures, I am going to address three types of situations in which an action of a company or manager not required by the law may prevent harm to a person or persons. The lectures will be structured around analysis of three cases that represent different aspects of the law-ethics relationship.

Lecture 1 — The Limits of Loyalty: A Question of Disclosure

Lecture 2 — When Rights Collide: The Dial-a-Porn Puzzle

Lecture 3 — The Meaning of Integrity: The Use of Proprietary Information

Perhaps a quotation from Alan Goldman sets the framework. He says,[1]

> The question is not whether people in business should observe legal limits, but whether they ought to recognize moral obligations beyond the requirements of law, when assumption of such obligations is incompatible with maximization of profit. Should managers sacrifice profits for moral reasons not incorporated in law, or can they assume

that pursuit of profit within legal limits will tend toward a more moral outcome?

I will again be addressing the old and persistent question of whether business firms have any moral responsibility beyond what the law requires, and, if so, what is the basis of that responsibility.

The theoretical context for the discussion that follows may be located in the corporate social responsibility debates of the 1970's and the moral agency debates of the 1980's. Readers (or auditors) familiar with business ethics literature will know the arguments on each side of these debates.

The Corporate Social Responsibility debate can be summarized as follows: On one side is the Milton Friedman position. In an oft-published article entitled, *The Social Responsibility of Business is to Increase its Profits*,[2] Friedman argues that expenditures on social good, whether the symphony or toxic waste, has at least three faults: (1) expenditures that reduce profits are taking away from legal owners, the stockholders, without their consent; (2) corporate executives are not elected to set public policy, and (3) corporate executives have no particular wisdom on what the public good is or should be.

Over against that view, which had and has strong support in business, is the view that a corporation should be judged on its moral performance as well as fiscal performance. Corporations have power, money, etc. and they do participate in the community. Thus the idea of good corporate citizen arose and has developed.

The moral agency debate of the 1980's centers on whether or not a corporation can have a conscience or can be held to any moral standard *as a corporation*. The terms and content of the discussion have changed in several important ways from the corporate social responsibility debate. In the latter, the question is whether corporations *should* involve their resources in improving the cultural and social life of the larger community (unless there is a direct public relations pay-off). In the current debate the question has changed from whether a corporation *should* be involved to whether a corporation, as distinct from individual managers, *can* be involved.[3]

Briefly, the moral agency debate can be summarized as follows:

— One side argues strongly that only individuals make decisions; that "conscience" cannot be ascribed to an institution; that individual wrong-doers can be held accountable for crimes, but not the whole organization. Support for the no-conscience position is made by pointing out that over time personnel in a firm change, and we can't hold new groups responsible for sins of past players. Also, many innocent people, including stockholders, would be hurt if institution's were held responsible.

vs.

— The argument that conscience can be ascribed to a corporation because there are identifiable decision making centers, e.g. the executive committee, the Board of Directors, and the strategic planning committee, that ponder, keep minutes, develop history, and, importantly, have responsibility to set policy and make decisions on behalf of the organization.

I will use this theoretical framework as the background in which I will develop my three lectures, but, I will address a different question. To repeat, what, if anything, is required of business firms beyond what the law prohibits or requires?

Notes

1. Goldman, Alan, "Business Ethics: Profits, Utilities, and Moral Rights," *Philosophy and Public Affairs* 9 No. 3, p. 261.

2. *New York Times Magazine*, Sept. 13, 1970, pp. 32-33.

3. For extended discussions and bibliographical suggestions on moral agency, see French, Peter, *Collective and Corporate Responsibility*, Columbia University Press, New York, 1984; May, Larry, *The Morality of Groups*, University of Notre Dame Press, Notre Dame, 1987; Regan, Tom, *Just Business*, Random House, New York, 1984; and Donaldson, Thomas, *Corporations and Morality*, Prentice Hall, Englewood Cliffs, N. J., 1982.

Lecture I

The Limits of Loyalty: A Question of Disclosure

In this first lecture, I will use a case involving disclosure or non-disclosure of a potential problem to the purchaser of a piece of commercial real estate. The case should be seen as symbolic or representative of a recurrent type of problem that business managers face.

Resort Properties

International Constructors, Inc. is a large international engineering and construction company. With major projects world-wide, ICI is also a major owner of real estate for their various operations. As their projects end or industry trends change, this real estate becomes surplus property. The disposition of this property is the responsibility of the corporate real estate manager, Joe Straightshooter.

One major piece of land was acquired by ICI over 10 years ago for use as a marina yard in a developing area of the U. S. Unfortunately, the off-shore work does not develop, and ICI was left holding 2,000 acres of rural property along the Atlantic Coast. As time passes, this area of the country begins to develop and the property increases in value. The highest—and best—use becomes resort property, and several developers begin making inquiries. A tentative deal is finally struck with the sole bidder, a major golf-course resort developer.

As final details are negotiated, Straightshooter is shown plans of the potential development. Of particular interest to Joe is the proposed density of dwellings. Joe is aware of a major drainage problem which has been caused over the years by adjacent industry. This blockage causes periodic flooding during heavy rains. Joe observes that a large number of condominium units are to be located in the area where the flooding occurs. As the density is a key determinant for the rather high sales price, Joe knows that eliminating these condominiums would significantly impact the price and perhaps cause the sale to collapse.

Due to a downturn in the industry and several quarters of red ink, significant pressure is being applied to Joe by upper-level management. ICI is not doing well financially and key executives want the property sold in order to improve the cash flow.

What should Joe do? Should he explain the drainage problem to the potential buyers?

Is withholding this information deception?

What ethical issue(s) does the case present?

The case raises at least two basic ethical issues

(1) What, if any, responsibility does the firm/manager have to the purchaser/developer?

(2) What, if any, responsibility does the firm/manager have to the condo buyers in case of flooding?

Ethical issues in business always (or almost always) involve profit vs. some other interest, such as the customer, the employee, the common good, or individual conscience. Profit, in our society, is itself taken as a good. Profit is a symbol that stands for return on investment to the stockholder, protection of jobs, creation of new jobs, the health of the economy, and reward and salary increases for employees and managers.

In *Resort Properties*, the tension between profit and other interests is exacerbated by the recent flow of red ink. The company's fiscal health and the preservation of jobs are in some jeopardy. For Joe, the problem of conscience is clear. If he says nothing about the flooding problem to the developer, he contributes to the fiscal health, or survival, of his firm — at least in the short run — and may save the jobs of some employees. Yet, he possesses knowledge of a condition that may cause severe harm to the developer or future condo purchasers.

To understand the intensity of Joe's dilemma, we need to remember that a basic principle in American business is loyalty to the firm. The literature and case studies on whistle blowers underscore how deeply ingrained loyalty is and the price to be paid for violating that loyalty. We have seen this in cases where threats to life and health are at stake, e. g. in toxic waste cases and the stories of the engineers at Morton Thiokol. For Joe, since "only" property damage is likely, there is no such urgency to support what may be perceived as disloyalty.

I am choosing this case because I have used it on at least 40 occasions in ethics seminars with managers in many different industries, including defense, telecommunications, and computer information systems. The discussion of the case has been very instructive, because it draws a great deal of difference of opinion, if not conflict, and is very useful in terms of revealing the relation of law and ethics, whether there is any moral obligation to protect end users against malfeasance or negligence by your customer, and whether professional knowledge creates a special obligation regardless of the law. The discussion and final vote tally are always instructive because they reveal how divided business managers are on these kinds of issues. It is precisely where there is divided opinion about what is ethical that more focus is needed.

In considering the case, it will be helpful to know

(1) that ICI, the seller, designs and constructs large buildings and building complexes

(2) that ICI is in serious financial trouble, business is down, that it has already gone through severe cost cutting, and that it is running in the red this year

and

(3) that the law in the state where the firm is located as well as the law in the state where the property is located do not require disclosure.

So with that as background, ask yourself, "What would you want your company to do if you were in that situation?"

In discussions of this case, a series of representative categories of responses have emerged. The consistent majority view is to sell and say nothing. That view is supported by an assertion of buyer beware or some variant, such as "let the rules of the market operate." I can safely report that in 1989 that buyer beware, or *caveat emptor*, is alive and well. Despite the steady move away from buyer beware since *MacPherson v. Buick*[1] in 1916, there is strong support for the doctrine. The prevailing mood that I find when I make the point that buyer beware has been severely weakened, if not overturned, is that we ought to reestablish it.

A second kind of support for selling without disclosure is that if it is legal it is alright. In part this is the Friedman argument, cited earlier; in part it is suggested that regulators or inspectors have the responsibility to insure safety before any project is approved.

Still another argument for disposing without disclosing is that the developer is a professional who can take care of himself. It is the developer's responsibility to perform geological surveys, or contract for them, and this absolves Joe and his firm from any disclosure requirement.

The minority view argues for full disclosure of the potential flooding problem to the developer. Some people argue that a seller of property should disclose a serious problem regardless of the law in order to protect the customer and prevent harm. (This is often followed up with a statement that "I might be the condo purchaser, and I would want to be protected.") Others argue forcefully that regardless of the present law, the firm will be subject to lawsuits in the future as the social climate changes. Prudence calls for disclosure.

The positions summarized above parallel the kinds of statements that the case has elicited in virtually every situation where it has been used. In the firm where the case originated, the vote of a group of managers was 45 to 15 to sell and say nothing. With one exception in the 40 or so uses that I have made of the case in business settings, the vote has been two to one to sell without disclosure.

Buyer beware, as a principle, consistently takes precedence over protecting either the developer or the condo purchasers against harm. Much of the support for saying nothing is based on the fact that the law does not require divulging the information about the possible flooding. As indicated previously, some of those who vote to disclose do so in order to avoid a future lawsuit.

Once again, the case raises the following basic issues:

What, if any, responsibility does the firm/manager have to the purchaser/developer?

What, if any, responsibility does the firm/manager have to the condo buyers in case of flooding?

In the analysis that follows, we will, first, look at the law of disclosure as it applies in business settings, second, look at the law on disclosure in the professions to see if there are helpful analogues, and then come back to *Resort Properties* with a conclusion.

We need to look at the law because it defines what we are required or permitted to do or prohibited from doing. Before we can examine Alan Goldman's question about whether businesses ought to recognize moral obligations beyond the law, we need to know what the legal limits are. We also need to understand why the limits have been set and what public policy—what moral position—they represent.

A recent law journal article on the duty to warn as it applies to therapists summarizes the basic law by saying, "Under the common law, there is no general duty to act to protect another from harm."[2] The basis for this position, as described in the Restatement of Torts, the Bible on tort law, is that knowing that one's action is necessary to protect another from harm does not impose a duty to take action.[3] Nonfeasance, passive inaction, is not the basis for legal liability.

The law does impose a duty to aid or protect in many circumstances, but such a duty is limited to situations in which there is a special relationship. Thus physicians have the responsibility to protect patients against the harmful effects of misused drugs, and automobile manufacturers must protect consumers from faulty brake systems. Specified duties are defined in virtually every profession and vocation. But the duty to aid or protect is limited to those restrictions or requirements established through case or statutory law.

What, then, do we learn from the law?

I. The Law of Disclosure on Unimproved Property

The property in question in *Resort Properties* is located in South Carolina. In 1981, in *Jackson v. River Pines, Inc.*,[4] ". . . the South Carolina Supreme Court declined to continue its movement away from the doctrine of *caveat emptor* in the sale of residential real estate. . .

The court held that an implied warranty of fitness for intended use does not spring from the sale of unimproved land upon which a new building is subsequently constructed and sold."[5] This decision has been cited in subsequent cases and is still the law in South Carolina.

Wilkins, in a 1982 law review article says that this is consistent with the majority of American jurisdictions that have considered the issue. In South Carolina, in the absence of fraud or misrepresentation, *caveat emptor* governs the obligations of the parties in the sale of real estate. ". . . the court indicated that in South Carolina, the purchaser of unimproved land must specifically covenant to protect whatever special rights or interests he expects to acquire in the land."[6]

There is an implied warranty for fitness for sale of a new building, but not for unimproved land. Why not? One reason is that future use is often not clearly defined, making it difficult or impossible to warrant fitness. But beyond that, the South Carolina court pointed out that the suitability of the land may be dependent upon architectural proposals entirely independent of the conveyance. Perhaps more important, the purchaser can fully inspect undeveloped land which renders denial of an implied warranty fair or just.[7]

For our case, let us assume that the applicable law parallels that of South Carolina. After all, even though the law in many areas is evolving and narrowing the limits of *caveat emptor*, there nonetheless remains that area where the doctrine still holds and our basic ethical question still remains.

If we apply the South Carolina position to our case, Joe Straightshooter and/or his company could make a strong argument that the purchaser, especially a developer, could make, indeed would be expected to make a thorough inspection before purchasing the property and certainly before proceeding to build. Again, if we look to *Jackson* as a precedent for our case, ICI would be protected from any recovery for damages by the developer or condo owners in the event that subsequent flooding caused damage.

Some jurisdictions have adopted stricter requirements for disclosure for both unimproved and improved property. As pointed out above, there is an implied warranty of fitness for sale of a new building in South Carolina. In contrast, California has a fairly strong disclosure requirement that applies to unimproved and improved property, but it is not clear that a seller in the *Resort Properties* case would be legally required to disclose even under that law.

California law states,[8]
The seller's real estate agent is under the same affirmative duty as his principal to disclose to the buyer facts materially affecting the value or desirability of the property that are known to him and which he knows are not known to, *or within the reach of the diligent attention and observation of, the buyer* . . . (emphasis added.)

The latest California commentary on *Real Estate Law* regarding disclosure declares that an agent has a more stringent duty to third persons than the fiduciary duty owed to the owner. The commentary says, "The agent cannot misrepresent the subject matter of the transaction, or utter 'half-truths', and he has a duty to disclose material defects in the subject matter. . ."[9]

For application to our analysis, we would need to ask if the potential flooding constitutes a 'material defect' (it certainly seems to) and, more seriously, if Joe Straightshooter says nothing is he uttering a half-truth. If we determine that Joe's silence does *not* constitute a half-truth, we then are back at our basic question as to Joe's moral responsibility when there is no legal requirement.

Again, in South Carolina, Joe's non-disclosure would certainly be lawful, and there is an explicit statement by the Court that the burden is on the *purchaser*.

II. The Law on Disclosure in Products Liability

One promising arena for exploration for establishing an obligation to disclose in *Resort Properties* or similar situations in business is in products liability. The brief history is that in a sixty year period, beginning with *MacPherson* v. *Buick* in 1916, the law has moved from a position of buyer beware to seller beware. Gradually, through a series of court cases that established new standards that became recognized in successive versions of the *Restatement of Torts*, negligence, reasonable foreseeability, and knowledge of a harm were all removed as requirements for recovery by injured plaintiffs. Two authors who review, somewhat despairingly, the increasingly stringent requirements for warnings in products liability development talk about "the establishment of a new hegemony in the law of product liability."[10] Among other public policy reasons that courts have used for moving toward strict liability in products manufacture and selling are the priority of compensation for injured victims and the expectation that more stringent requirements would promote public safety and provide incentives for manufacturing safer products.

Citations on failure to warn in cases dealing with products concentrate heavily on drugs, from prescriptions to eye drops, toxic substances and toxic waste, and heavy machinery. But, the most recent edition of the *Products Liability Reporter*[11] lists cases on everything from bottle capping to hammers to infant incubators to propane gas to pizza dough roller machines.

(Perhaps the most troubling citation to me was "book, defective ideas." When I checked out the Michigan case to which the quote referred, I was relieved to find that it was a suit against a publisher of a how-to book on various kinds of repair equipment. The publisher was not held liable to test all of the equipment included in the book. But, should professors be held responsible for defective ideas? Who, other than the Vatican, can judge whether an idea is defective?)

What do we learn from products liability law that may have wider application in terms of any principle regarding the obligation of a business firm to disclose potential harm? Certainly we learn that the law has moved substantially toward protecting consumers against harm, even to the extent of diluting if not removing negligence or foreseeability. If we were able to base any general obligation to protect against (potential) harm on products liability law, we could establish an extensive standard of disclosure.

There are important limitations to product liability and its possible application to the broader situation, though, that provide a basis for caution. Some considerations are the following:

• Type of Harm — The harm against which protection is given, whether lawn darts or apparel pins, is directed to protection against physical injury or death. The well-known cases, such as Manville and asbestos and A. H. Robins and the Dalkon shield, all deal with *serious* threats to health and life. Indeed, short of fraud or deceit (or possibly negligence), businesses that "manufacture" and sell products that involve financial risk, e. g. limited partnerships which invest in apartments, office buildings, or mobile home parks, are not held to the strict liability standard.

• Sophisticated User Defense — The liability of a manufacturer or seller of a potentially dangerous product may be limited if there is a knowledgeable intermediary standing between the initial seller and injured user. In many situations, the end users would not be known and, in any event, in the case of industrial purchasers/employers, the end users are under the control of or much more accessible to the employer.

The thrust of the current status of this defense, as assessed in a 1988 *Virginia Law Review* article,[12] is such that it would protect the firm in *Resort Property* from liability to condo purchasers in the event of flood *if* the flood condition were communicated to the developer/purchaser. So if we were to extend this defense to the property disposition situation, clear notice to the developer would be required.

There is more that we can learn from analysis of the sophisticated user defense. The public policy behind the defense has at least two goals, prevention of injury *and* the encouragement of efficient decision making.

Presumably, if a user of a product is aware of actual or potential defects prior to purchase, that knowledge will affect either the decision to buy or the use of the product, or both. If we apply this reasoning to *Resort Properties*, it helps to clarify the situation as well as suggests that disclosure should be made. The only reason not to disclose is that it may delay or terminate the sale to the developer, either of which are harmful to ICI in its quest for immediate cash flow. In a products liability case, though, protecting the interest of the manufacturer/seller would not be a legitimate basis to withhold information about potential dangers from a purchaser.

What, if any, essential difference is there between the sale of a manufactured item and undeveloped property that protects the seller of property from the same standard of disclosure as the manufacturer?

One further comment is in order. In the assessment of current law, there is a suggestion from a Federal court that even the duty to warn an intermediary is eliminated when the intermediary is already knowledgeable. Indeed, there are several decisions that suggest that "sellers avoid liability completely if the intermediary is knowledgeable, regardless of whether the intermediary acquired its knowledge from a warning by the seller or some other source." That seems to say that specific knowledge is acquired by the purchaser, but it might be extended to presumed knowledge due to experience. As noted earlier, one reason given for not disclosing in *Resort Properties* is that the developer would be expected to do tests and that regulatory bodies would discover the problem if the developer failed to do so. Is it possible to expand "when the intermediary is knowledgeable" to "when the intermediary *should* be knowledgeable?" That would reduce the duty to warn.

Our question, in part, has been whether there is an obligation, or duty, to warn in *Resort* type cases. We should be aware that duty as a category has been criticized as a "conclusionary determination. . ."[13] Indeed a major commentary on torts joins those who criticize duty as a useful category, saying that in addition to duty being a "shorthand statement of a conclusion," duty is "only an expression of the sum total of those considerations of policy which lead the law to say that the plaintiff is entitled to its protection."[14] Perhaps what we are examining is whether in cases like *Resort* there are policy considerations that lead developer/purchasers to be entitled to legal protection. We shall need to examine such policy considerations in our concluding section.

• Learned Intermediary Rule — Another legal doctrine that may be useful for our analysis is that of the "learned intermediary."[15] This doctrine is especially applicable to ethical drugs (prescription drugs) because a physician, who is knowledgeable about both the drug and the patient, stands between the manufacturer and the user. The requirement for the manufacturer to use the learned intermediary defense, though, is that the manufacturer has adequately warned the physician about the drug.

If we were to apply the principle of the learned intermediary to the seller of property in *Resort*, the company would be absolved of liability to the condo purchasers in the event of flood if warning about the potential flooding had been given to the developer. Certainly a developer is not seen as having the same skill and training as a physician, nor does the developer have the kind of knowledge about and close relation with a patient as does a physician (although the change in the nature of the physician/patient relation may be moving closer to that of developer/condo purchaser in our present climate).

Nonetheless, the principle and its recognition as a legitimate legal defense leads to two tentative conclusions as applied to *Resort Properties*: (1) that ICI would be absolved of responsibility to the condo purchasers if it provided adequate warning to the developer/purchaser and (2) that warning about the potential flooding should be given to the developer purchaser.

• No Need for Warning — Although most of the discussion of the current state of the law indicates there is a requirement of a warning of a defect at least to an intermediary that is sophisticated or learned, there is at least some case law that might support a contention that ICI has no duty to disclose the potential flooding. In a 1984 ruling in *Cruz v Texaco*,[16] a products liability case involving a used winch truck, a Federal court held that knowledge on the part of the purchaser of the danger of driving a winch truck with certain loads, coupled with a driver training program, removed any duty of the seller to warn the driver. The decision cites the Restatement of Torts (S 388) which says that a seller is liable, among other reasons, if the seller "has no reason to believe that those for whose use the chattel is supplied will realize its dangerous condition. . . ."[17]

The reasoning contained in the decision in *Cruz* could be extended to the *Resort* case by focusing on the expected knowledge and experience of the developer. This indeed is what a number of respondents to the case have done in virtually every discussion in corporate seminars.

We need to ask whether the land transfer is similar, that is, whether any obligation that ICI has is transferred or absolved because of the presumed knowledge of the developer and whether we agree with the reasoning in *Cruz*.

III. The Law on Disclosure in Other Areas

Psychiatry — Tarasoff and the psychotherapists duty to warn.

One of the most discussed duty to warn situations is that of the therapist when a patient threatens violent acts against a third party. In brief, in 1976 the California Supreme Court established for the first time a duty for therapists to warn third parties of threatened violence. That standard has subsequently been adopted in most other jurisdictions.

The situation presented to the Court in *Tarasoff v. Regents of the University of California*[18] was one in which a patient told a University psychologist that he would kill a young woman if she continued her refusal to marry him. Although the threat was reported to the campus police, no attempt was made to warn the woman. The campus police interviewed and dismissed the patient, since he apparently posed no immediate harm. Subsequently he stabbed the woman to death.

The important thing for our discussion is the basis on which the court extended the duty to warn for therapists. At the heart of the decision was the fact that a special relationship exists between a therapist and patient which created an obligation, or duty, on the part of the therapist to warn third parties. Opponents of the *Tarasoff* decision have argued that the special relationship creates a prior duty to the patient and that the traditional privilege of confidentiality should be maintained. Indeed, the unique thing about *Tarasoff* is that it limited confidentiality when third parties were threatened. The Court obviously saw the protection of third parties as being of greater importance than confidentiality or any damage that disclosure might do to the therapist-patient relation.

What guidance does *Tarasoff* provide to us in the property sale situation presented in *Resort Properties*? I think very little. *Tarasoff* establishes a duty to warn in cases of threats of violence because of a special relationship between therapist and patient. In *Resort* the relationship of a potential purchaser of property to the seller does not qualify on any grounds as a "special relationship" which creates obligations to either the developer or the prospective condo purchasers. Moreover, the duty to warn in *Tarasoff* is limited to situations in which there is a threat of violence or serious physical harm. That kind of harm does not exist in *Resort* where it is anticipated that if there is any damage it will be to property.

Is *Tarasoff* of any possible use to us then beyond negating any application of the special relationship principle? Possibly. The therapist in *Tarasoff* possessed professional knowledge, that is, knowledge gained as the result of special training and experience. Does the kind of professional knowledge that ICI's sales agent has create a special burden with a resultant duty to warn? We will hold that question in abeyance for now, but return to it later after the consideration of other cases.

Consideration of the duty to warn on the part of therapists leads to reflection about other professional relations and prevailing standards.

One of the most discussed issues currently is whether or not physicians and other health professionals should disclose that a patient has AIDS or is HIV positive to third parties, especially to spouses. Although objections have been raised to any reporting, even to State agencies, on the prudential grounds that the threat of reporting will scare off real or potential AIDS victims, a serious argument has been waged about whether there is a duty to warn spouses or lovers. In the summer of 1988, after heated discussion, the AMA voted that physicians indeed have an obligation to warn spouses when an AIDS patient refuses to do so.

This step by the AMA extended the limitations on physician-patient confidentiality. Over the years, limits to confidentiality to the patient have been developed in the case of a suspected felony (public order), a contagious disease (public health), pilots and drivers of public conveyances (public good) and child abuse (society's obligation to protect children). The newly adopted duty to warn in the case of AIDS is specifically directed to protecting a victim's spouse. Such a duty to the spouse does not exist in the case of a patient with syphilis or some other venereal disease, much less an illness like influenza. The distinctive thing about AIDS is that it is a death threat and there is no known cure.

The point of the above for our discussion is that there are specified situations in the medical arena where there is a duty to warn. It is important to note, though, that the situations where the duty exists is limited to situations in which what is perceived as an overwhelming threat to society or continued violence or death to identified individuals exists.

In the case of both the physician and the therapists what we really see is very strong moral and legal support for maintaining confidentiality. The restrictions are limited in number and scope, and extensions of the duty to warn, whether imposed by the court as in *Tarasoff* or by a professional society as with the AMA and AIDS, are added grudgingly and seldom.

In sum, we will not find support for establishing a duty to warn in a *Resort Property* type case from the health professions. But we may find something else of importance to our exploration. We need to ask, "Why in the case of physicians and therapists, as well as for other professionals such as attorneys, clergy, and journalists, is confidentiality so well protected in the law?" What we find is that there are other interests that are served, such as due process, free speech, and privacy that society values more than that which could be gained in disclosure in the context of certain professional relationships. The duty to warn is limited in these relationships precisely because it is important to protect privacy and fairness, on the one hand, and encourage people to utilize professional help, on the other hand.

Thus, society forgoes certain benefits that might be derived from disclosure in order to protect other interests.

Question: Is there any social good in non-disclosure in a situation such as that presented in *Resort Properties* that parallels those things that support confidentiality over against disclosure?

In a sense we have two questions, or one question that can be approached in two ways. If we ask why a company should disclose a potential harm when not legally required to do so, the burden is on those who call for disclosure. If we turn the question and ask why a company should not disclose a potential harm, the burden is on those who would limit disclosure.

One further thing needs to be noted about required disclosure by physicians and therapists. In every case in which reporting is required, one or more lives is endangered or there is the threat of serious physical violence or contagious disease. Moreover, the threats need to be identifiable and real; in the case of the therapist and notifying a spouse about AIDS there is a specific threatened individual. Bodily safety, health, and life take precedence over confidentiality. The limitation of disclosure to situations where there is such dire consequences is further reason to set aside any parallels to required disclosure by professionals to a situation where there will be serious financial harm through property damage.

• Professional Engineers — Engineers, especially those in involved in design and construction, provide a promising area of inquiry. Indeed, in the Code of

Ethics of the IEEE,[19] the major professional society covering construction, there is a clear statement about responsibility to the public. The first statement in the code talks about the engineer's obligation to the employer. The second statement defines an obligation to the public to protect safety. There is then a line that says that this second obligation takes priority over the first.

Although the analog from the engineers may be promising, there are at least two limiting factors: (1) it is quite possible that Joe Straightshooter is neither an engineer nor the member of any like professional society with a similar code of ethics, and (2) the situations in which engineers usually get into reporting to the public involve a direct threat to life and limb, an element lacking in *Resort Properties.*

Nonetheless, the fact that there is the recognition by a professional society that obligations to protect the public take precedence over loyalty to the employer in certain circumstances, even though not required in law, is one example of a perceived ethical obligation to which we will want to return.

Where else can we turn for useful analogies?

• Accountants — There are several possible lessons to be drawn from accountants for our analysis. The American Institute of Certified Public Accountants (AICPA)[20] the largest of the professional societies for accountants, has a well developed code of ethics. Although public accountants, especially the Big Eight firms, have tended to be the leaders in the profession and receive the most public attention, almost half of the

members of the AICPA work for private firms as internal auditors or some other management function.
According to the AICPA, its standards apply to all
members, whatever their professional location.

Public accountants have as their most important function disclosure about their clients to the public. On the
basis of their analysis of the fiscal health of their clients,
they develop financial reports that are used by investors,
lenders, and regulatory agencies who have or may have
dealings with the client.

Here we see the first clear instance of reporting of
possible *financial harm*, whereas other situations have
all involved physical injury or death.

The obvious problem with the public accountant as
model is that everyone, the client, the accountant, and
the public knows and expects that the reporting will
occur. The public accountant has *independence* as the
first principle governing professional activity.

The important thing for our analysis, though, is that
the AICPA maintains that its code of ethics applies to
all members, wherever they are situated. Thus the
accountant who is an employee or a manager of a business firm still has the obligation, according to the code,
to report certain things to the public. In practice,
though, that which is to be reported is generally limited
to fraud or other criminal behavior, not to information
on every possible event that might lead to financial
harm to investors, lenders, or other users of company
financial reports. In recent years, though, there has
been increasing pressure from the courts, the Congress,
and the SEC to have accountants play a larger role in
protecting the public against financial harm. This is

especially the case where there is fraud, but in celebrated instances of large losses due to extremely risky ventures there has been intensified pressure for accountants to disclose such risks to regulators and the public. Both Congress and the courts have begun to push accountants to perform a "public watchdog" role to protect users of their reports against financial loss.

It is those situations that do not involve fraud that are the most instructive for our analysis. Beyond that, the National Association of Accountants, the professional organization of accountants who work within business, has recently adopted a code of ethics in which it calls for reporting in certain instances. The code is rather timid in limiting the reporting to the board of directors as a last resort, but it does establish the principle that a manager does have responsibilities beyond those to his or her management.

Now, let's go back to our case. What have we learned from the products liability law and the law in the professions about whether Joe Straightshooter should disclose? Does Joe have a duty to act?

• The Duty to Act

It is clear that there is a legally prescribed duty to act to prevent harm in many situations, including the protection of third parties by professionals which we discussed earlier. Equally clear, short of a specific legal requirement to the contrary, one is not held liable for failure to act to prevent harm in many situations where one is not the cause of the harm. As stated earlier, the common law holds one liable for malfeasance, not nonfeasance.

An interesting argument for our analysis of *Resort Properties* is put forward by Marshall Shapo in a book entitled, *The Duty to Act*. Shapo states his thesis as follows,[21]

> ... that persons who can use energy, ability, or information to aid others in serious peril without significant inconvenience or harm to themselves should do so.

In the book, Shapo analyzes present law in a large range of situations in which harm may befall someone from another's action or inaction. He organizes the work according to types of social relationships and further divides his analysis into private and public relationships. Business dealings fall under the private heading, and what he has to say would apply both to Joe Straightshooter and his firm, ICI.

Important to our analysis is the basis he uses for ascribing a duty. In his reading of tort law, a central element is the exercise and default of the use of power. So he moves to develop a "principal hypothesis that power relationships provides meaningful explanations of desirable results. . . ."[22] Control and submission, power and dependence — transactional superiority in one party — characterize many relationships where liability is assigned in law. Beyond that, liability is often imposed, as he sees it, for reasons that blend humanitarian concern with efficiency factors. The humanitarian element, along with considerations of fairness, may produce results that are more "persuasive to the community."

After reviewing a complex set of relationships, including those in business, in which there is power and control by one party, Shapo concludes,[23]

> I have evolved as a working principle that one has a duty to aid others in situations in which hazardous conditions necessitate assistance for the preservation of life and of physical integrity, and in which one possesses the power to expend energy in that task without serious inconvenience or possibility of harm to himself.

That statement is promising for looking for support for establishing a duty to aid, but what we have so far is limited only to life and physical integrity. If Shapo said no more, then we would need to extend his thesis or recognize that it would not apply to our case. He goes a step further, though, when he continues the quoted passage with,[24]

> . . . I have suggested that this duty, vindicable by tort judgements, also should apply on occasion to the protection of other vital personal interests in relations of transactional superiority and helpless dependence.

Regrettably, the examples that Shapo gives, even in the employment situation involve physical injury. Thus, we will have to make a sound argument for using the second quoted statement as the basis for making a case of disclosure in instances of real or potential financial harm.

Before leaving our assessment of the law in business and the professions as it applies to our case, it may be well to mention at least two other avenues that might be pursued in a longer exploration.

• Causation

The concept of causation in the law has been and is subject to continuous discussion among philosophers of law and has major implications for tort law. This is certainly the case with strict liability, but philosophers continue to discuss the relation of causation and liability as it applies to many other situations involving harm. Two recent examples of this, representing different if not opposing viewpoints, are that of Judith Jarvis Thomson[25] and Fischer and Ennis[26] in response to Thomson. Thomson essentially argues that liability ought to be associated with causation, even if the line is blurred in cases such as multiple manufacturers of DES with no traceable tie to an injured victim. The contrasting position argues that liability is to be shared among the actual harm-causer and anyone who acted negligently toward the victim.

• Harming

Another possible line of discussion relates to positive and negative duties and how that applies to harming through failure to act. Frances Myrna Kamm (1986)[27] examines this topic in a very interesting way by looking at the claim that Rachels and others make that there is a moral equivalent between killing and letting die and seeing if that extends to harming and not aiding when there is less than life at stake.

The argument is very complex, involving such things as whether the harm involves physical intrusiveness and whether the party harmed had a right to that which is denied. For our case, one question would be whether the developer had a moral right to the information about potential harm even though he did not have a legal right.

Conclusion
So what do I propose as the resolution to the case?

I will argue that Joe and/or ICI should disclose the potential flood problem to the developer. The grounds for reaching that conclusion are several and complex, but the process includes drawing from some of the earlier discussion of legal concepts and analogies.

• Professional Knowledge

Joe Straightshooter is the manager at ICI charged with the sale of the property. Although we are not certain of his training and experience, ICI is confident enough in him to delegate sale of the land to him. Moreover, the information revealed in the case indicates that he knows the property well enough to detect that the placement of the condos puts them in jeopardy in the event of flood.

In the case of professionals who are required to disclose information, it is their professional knowledge and judgment that leads to the requirement that they disclose. Psychiatrists are (presumably) able to judge when a patient's threat of violence toward a third party is serious or not. Physicians have the professional knowledge to determine if a patient has a communicable disease or if a child has been abused. Design engineers have the capability to detect flaws in fuel integrity systems, as in the Ford Pinto, and in o-rings, as in the Challenger.

It is the professional judgment that they make about what they learn in the context of their work that gives them the obligation to disclose. Joe Straightshooter is similarly placed. He has knowledge that has come to him because of his position and training. He is able to detect the potential problem. Furthermore, as with the professionals, Joe is in a position such that if he does not disclose the problem, it may go undetected until someone is harmed.

Two problems: (1) Joe is dealing with a developer who should be knowledgeable enough to search the records regarding the property and contract for geological surveys. Regardless, the local planning board, zoning board, or state engineer will need to give approvals and stands as a further professional gatekeeper. (2) The most likely danger from the flooding will be financial loss to the developer and/or condo owners. In the case of the psychiatrist, physician, and design engineer, loss of life is a likely result of non-disclosure.

I think that the problems can be met, or minimized, in the following way. The professionals are required to disclose regardless of what further interventions there may be. The syphilitic patient may be treated by another physician; the mentally disturbed patient may be treated by another psychiatrist before committing an act of violence. The requirement for professionals to disclose is certainly based on a serious danger to others, but the duty is not based on any requirement of last resort. Although it is true that more reporting requirements may be found for potential danger to health and life over against property, accountants have the responsibility of disclosing financial risks and there are disclosure laws for real estate agents who deal with improved real property, even in South Carolina.

Thus, I think that professional knowledge carries with it a special burden, and it will serve as a central basis on which to build a case for disclosure in *Resort Properties*.

* No Countervailing Good

We need to ask why in the case of physicians and therapists, as well as for other professionals such as attorneys, clergy, and journalists, confidentiality is so well protected in the law. What we find is that there are other interests that are served, such as due process, free speech, and privacy that society values more than that which could be gained in disclosure in the context of certain professional relationships. The duty to warn is limited in these relationships precisely because it is important to protect privacy and fairness, on the one hand, and encourage people to utilize professional help, on the other hand. Thus, society forgoes certain benefits that might be derived from disclosure in order to protect other interests.

Question: What is the social good in non-disclosure in a situation such as that presented in *Resort Properties* that parallels those things that support confidentiality over against disclosure?

The most obvious "good" to be protected by non-disclosure are the values that inhere in free markets and unrestrained trade. It can be argued that reporting requirements clearly act as an impediment to buying and selling and the free flow of capital. Yet, I will argue that protection of these interests is not on the same level as those interests we protect with professional confidentiality.

Simply put, physicians, psychiatrists, attorneys, clergy, and journalists could not perform valuable social functions without confidentiality. Such is not the case in buying and selling. One only needs to look to products liability and the way in which manufacturers have adjusted to the radical shift from *caveat emptor* to strict liability to see that more stringent obligations to protect the consumer have not destroyed nor seriously impaired business. The societal interest represented in shifting the burden to the producer to insure safety, as well as the disclosure requirements in improved real estate, indicate a steady shift in recent decades to protect consumers at whatever cost that may mean to commerce.

• Professional Responsibility

The recognition by a professional society representing engineers that obligations to protect the public take precedence over loyalty to the employer in certain circumstances, even though not required in law, is an important model for our analysis.

Professional engineers have many similarities to a manager like Joe Straightshooter. Engineers tend to be employed by large firms, they carry out rather than make policy and, through education and experience, they are able to perceive potential dangers to consumers and users of company products.

Despite the fact that Joe Straightshooter may not be a "professional," in the formal sense of that word, the fact that he was able to perceive the potential flooding places him in an analogous position to a design engineer or quality assurance officer. Joe may lack the authority of a quality assurance officer to hold up delivery of a product, thus the completion of a sale, but he has the same capability of preventing harm to the customer.

• The Duty to Act
The argument that Marshall Shapo makes for the duty to act provides a very promising avenue for concluding that Joe Straightshooter or ICI should report the flooding problem.

Again, his statement was,[28]

> . . . that persons who can use energy, ability, or information to aid others in serious peril without significant inconvenience or harm to themselves should do so.

Although he qualified that duty with the phrase, "in relations of transactional superiority and helpless dependence," I see no reason to establish such a limit. Again, I would cite professional engineers, quality assurance officers, and public accountants who are often dealing with customers or users who could hardly be classified as "helpless" or "dependent" and still have a duty to disclose.

• Objections – There are at least two major arguments that are consistently made in the type of case presented by *Resort Properties* that warrant brief comment.

• Learned Intermediary – A strong argument can be made that a developer is, or should be, knowledgeable about how to discover real or potential geological problems prior to purchase of property.

Yet, a knowledgeable purchaser does not stand as a bar to liability in many other situations. Even though the air force or airlines, with trained inspectors and engineers, are the intended purchasers of aircraft, the manufacturer has the responsibility to warrant the safety of their product *and* to notify the purchaser if a problem is detected after delivery.

The learned intermediary rule is a defense against liability to an injured third party, e.g. the user of a prescription drug, only if full information about potential dangers has been provided to the physician who prescribes the drug. In analogous fashion, ICI would presumably be protected from any liability to the condo owners in the event of flood only if it had fully disclosed the flooding problem to the purchaser.

Nonetheless, the principle and its recognition as a legitimate legal defense lead to two tentative conclusions as applied to *Report Property*: (1) that ICI would be absolved of responsibility to the condo purchasers if it provided adequate warning to the developer/purchaser and (2) that warning about the potential flooding should be given to the developer purchaser.

• Competitive Disadvantage — Another argument often raised in discussions of corporate social responsibility is that of competitive disadvantage if a firm does that beyond what the law requires. A common illustration is that if one refinery invests in scrubbers to reduce pollutants while competitors are not, that the refinery that acts will either lose business from higher prices or profits from higher costs.

The point must be granted.

There are two responses, though: (1) the determination of what action is ethical is regardless of whether it is cost-free and (2) that if installing scrubbers or disclosing potential flooding is "the right thing to do," the law should be changed to meet that standard. Individual firms may have to pay a cost until the law catches up.

Thus, it is my contention that professional knowledge carries with it the duty to protect innocent parties unless there is a countervailing social good that takes precedence. Despite the protection that existing law may provide to firms like ICI which choose not to disclose potentially serious defects, there is a moral obligation to disclose that transcends the law.

Notes

1. *MacPherson v. Buick Motor Co.*, 111 N. E. 1050 (N. Y. 1916).

2. Salter, Dianne S., "The Duty to Warn Third Parties: a Retrospective on Tarasoff," (Case Note) 18 *Rutgers Law Journal*, Fall, 1985, pp. 145-164.

3. *RESTATEMENT (Second) OF TORTS* # 314 (1974).

4. *Jackson v. River Pines, Inc.*, 276 S. C. 29, 274 S. E. 2d 912 (1981).

5. Wilkens, Samuel L., "Caveat Emptor - Sale of Unimproved Land," (Annual Survey of South Carolina Law), 34 *South Carolina Law Review*, Aug., 1982, pp. 193-195.

6. *Ibid.*, p. 194.

7. *Ibid.*, p. 195. Wilkens notes that in North Carolina the law would require disclosure in undeveloped property of the kind we are dealing with in our case. This difference in adjacent states not only demonstrates the need to look closely at the law but, more importantly, the limitations of relying on the law as a moral guide. Certainly we would not argue that non-disclosure is immoral in North Carolina but moral in South Carolina.

8. *Current Law of Real Estate Law*, 1 Cal RE Rev, Part 2, # 4.14, p. 68.

9. *Real Estate Law* (Commentary), 1987.

10. Barry, Desmond T., Jr. and Edward Charles De Vito, "The Evolution of Warnings: The Liberal Trend Toward Absolute Product Liability," 20 *Forum* Fall, 1984, p. 43.

11. *Products Liability Reporter, 1986-1987.*

12. Willner, Kenneth M., "Failures to Warn and the Sophisticated User Defense," 74 *Virginia Law Review*, April 1988, pp. 579-607.

13. *Ibid.*, p. 593.

14. Prosser, W. and W. Keeton, *The Law of Torts*, 96, at 686 (5th ed. 1984), cited in Willner, *Ibid.*, p. 593-4.

15. Flannagan, Barbara Pope, "Products Liability: The Continued Viability of the Learned Intermediary Rule As It Applies to Product Warnings For Prescription Drugs," 20 *University of Richmond Law Review* Winter, 1986, pp. 405-423.

16. 589 F Supp 777 (S. D. Ill., 1984).

17. *Ibid.*

18. *Tarasoff v. Regents of University of California*, 17 Cal 3d 425, 551 P 2d 334, 131 *Cal Rptr* 14 (1976).

19. Code of Ethics of IEEE, the major professional association of engineers.

20. AICPA Code of Ethics

21. Shapo, Marshall S., *The Duty to Act*, University of Texas Press, Austin, 1977.

22. *Ibid.*, p. xiii.

23. *Ibid.*, p. 69.

24. *Ibid.*, p. 69.

25. Thompson, Judith Jarvis, "Remarks on Causation and Liability," *Philosophy and Public Affairs*, Vol. 13, No. 2, Spring, 1984, pp. 101-133.

26. Fischer, John Martin and Robert H. Ennis, "Causation & Liability," *Philosophy and Public Affairs*, Vol. 15, No. 1, Winter, 1986, pp. 33-40.

27. Kamm, Frances Myrna, "Harming, Not Aiding, and Positive Rights," *Philosophy and Public Affairs*, Winter, 1986, Vol. 15, No. 1, pp. 3-32.

28. Shapo, *op. cit.*, p. 69.

Lecture 2

When Rights Collide: The Dial-a-Porn Puzzle

I have chosen Dial-a-Porn as the topic for my second lecture because it dramatically focuses our attention on a very different aspect of whether business firms have obligations beyond those legally mandated.

Differences between the cases:
In *Resort Properties*, the focal case in lecture one, the immediate problem was that of possible financial harm to a purchaser due to failure to disclose a potential harm by an owner who may have been the sole possessor of knowledge about the harm. Although there were possible intervenors from state agencies and future Condo owners who might suffer future harm, the immediate and most pressing problem involved two parties. In some senses, since both were in business and presumed to be knowledgeable about the sale of property, they were on the popular "level playing field." Indeed, it may be argued that the developer might be expected to be more knowledgeable about unimproved property that the seller or its employee.

In contrast to the above, the 976 Porn case is extremely complex and involves many actors and affected parties. One basic difference in 976 Porn is that the potential harm may be both financial and psychological and knowledge about the problem is widely known by many agents who have the capability of acting. Second, whereas a decisive preventive action was available to the property owner in *Resort Properties*, the telephone companies have argued, with some justification, that they have been blocked by State and Federal regulatory agencies and by Federal courts from taking action to terminate 976 porn. Third, in *Resort Properties*, the potentially injured party, the developer, was an adult with presumed competence to protect himself. In 976 Porn, certainly the children and possibly the parents lack the knowledge of the harm and the ability to protect against it.

It should be noted that in the last year, there has been some Federal legislation that outlaws interstate dial-a-porn and some companies have instituted blocking — thus part of the problem has been resolved. Nonetheless, the case as a model of this kind of situation is still valuable, and there are major conflicts still remaining in some states, e. g. California. Moreover, the 1988 Federal legislation is being challenged in court on first amendment grounds.

Parallels between the cases:

There are also some parallels between the cases. In property sales, some commentators, and some state courts, hold that it is the purchaser that is responsible for inspecting unimproved property. In a similar vein, the phone companies, along with some commentators, have argued that it is the customer, the parents, who are responsible for controlling use of the phone. In *Resort*

Properties, ICI did not cause the flooding problem, but they could take action to prevent it. In 976-Porn, the telephone companies did not create nor market the dial-a-porn messages, but, at least in the eyes of some of their critics, could and should have taken some steps to limit or eliminate it.

Dial-a-Porn

It is 1985—you are a member of the executive committee of one of the Baby Bells—e. g. Southwestern Bell or Pacific Bell—and you have just been called to a meeting to discuss the company's position on dial-a-porn.

You know from the public relations department that there has been a flood of phone calls and letters protesting the "surprise" phone bills running from several hundred to $2,000 in a single month and a public interest group and a local evangelical ministers group has been denouncing pornography coming into the home via telephones—and demanding action by your company. The local ACLU has been almost as vocal as the protesters in its support of the right of individuals to listen to whatever they want in the privacy of their home. You also know from your chief financial officer that dial-a-porn has been bringing in at least $1 million per month in revenues.

At the meeting, you receive the following additional information: Congress passed a law in 1983 outlawing obscene or indecent communication for commercial purposes to any person under 18 years of age or any other person without that person's consent. The FCC has tried to block interstate dial-a-porn through regulation, but its proposed regulations have been struck down by the courts because they were overly broad and violated the first amendment. Your state Public Utilities Commission has refused to allow you to discriminate against any licensee to a 976 service line unless the message was illegal. Finally, you are told that it is permissible for you to terminate all 976 services, such as finance, weather, prayers and sports, but that put together they also bring in $1 million dollars in revenue each month.

Two questions:

1) What would you want your company to do if it had freedom of action?

2) What would you advise that the company do under the circumstances described?

As we begin to examine the issues posed by dial-a-porn, we should be aware of the complexity of the situation due to the large number of "actors" involved. There are legislative, judicial, and regulatory bodies at both Federal and State levels; there are regional and national telephone companies, each with its own directors and management; there are public interest groups reflecting a variety of points of view; and there are rights or rights claims put forward on behalf of children, telephone customers, pornographers, and adult users of pornography. Deciding what to do in the case, as well as determining what companies should do in these kinds of situations requires sorting out levels of responsibility as well as the competing rights. The issue is further complicated by the variety of views taken on the harmfulness of pornography.

History

The history of why and how the dial-a-porn issue arose is instructive and provides an important context for our analysis. Prior to 1983, special services such as time, weather, and sportsphone, were obtained from outside contractors, but under direct control of the local telephone company. On January 1, 1983, as part of the deregulation of the telephone system, the FCC prohibited the telephone operating companies, still part of the Bell System from providing "enhanced services" except through fully separate subsidiaries. The companies didn't want to establish new subsidiaries; thus this opened the door for dial-a-porn for the first time. Manufacturers of pornography applied for, and secured, 976 numbers along with contractors for the existing services.[1]

Almost immediately, Congressional efforts to eliminate dial-a-porn began. This interest on the part of Congress was not new. Indeed, the Federal legislative history on trying to limit pornography over the telephone can be traced back to the Communications Act of 1934. In 1968, the Act was amended with the addition of Section 233 which prohibited "obscene, lewd, lascivious, filthy, or indecent Communications by means of telephone."[2] That seemed adequate protection until the 1983 deregulation of the telephone system encouraged new providers to develop dial-a-porn.

Apparently the FCC was not certain that the 1968 amendment covered dial-a-porn. Accordingly, Congress again amended the Act and changed Section 233 to make it a crime to make "any obscene or indecent communication for commercial purposes to any person under 18 years of age or to any other person without that person's consent."[3] Although this was intended to close a loophole by addressing telephonic porn directly, some critics say that it legalized dial-a-porn for the first time. As a representative of Citizens of Decency through Law put it, "For the first time in the history of this country, obscene material was decriminalized for 'consenting adults'."[4]

If that indeed was the result, it was certainly not intended. Since 1983, members of Congress have been trying to put more restrictions on dial-a-porn. In that same period, the FCC has tried to fashion regulations which would prohibit access by children, but each time the regulations have been struck down as overly broad because of the limitations on free expression. Perhaps out of frustration at the failure to protect against access by children, Representative Bliley introduced the Telephone Decency act in March, 1987. His purpose was to prohibit "the transmission of obscene and indecent Communications for commercial purposes by means of telephone to any person, *regardless of age*."[5] (emphasis added)

January 1, 1984, is another landmark date in the development and proliferation of dial-a-porn. 1/1/84 marks the break up of the Bell System and the beginning of the Baby Bells, along with the entrance of many new long distance telephone companies. The divestiture decree breaking up A. T. & T. contained the restrictions on what was essentially monopoly control of

976 services before 1983. Responsibility for dealing with problems that developed was spread among regional companies, struggling to define their purposes and identities, and regulation became more diffuse as state public utility commissions began to exercise more control. For example, early in its new independent status, Pacific Bell introduced a tariff in which it proposed to exclude pornographers, but this was rejected by the California Public Utilities Commission. Apparently the Commission did not want to use regulation to limit free speech.

During the period from 1984 to 1988, Congressional efforts to pass limiting legislation continued, but concerns over free speech delayed action. The FCC made two tries to control dial-a-porn, but each time the regulations were struck down in court. The courts continually supported first amendment rights for various reasons. Thus the situation became more complex and charged as time went on without an acceptable resolution.

A sample of statements by two prominent senators on some of the legislation proposed during this period will show the complexity and intensity of the debate. The quotations also point out the basic conflict between protecting children from harm and protecting free speech. In early 1987, Senator Jesse Helms introduced a bill to help prevent rape and other sexual violence by prohibiting dial-a-porn operations. He said, in part, [6]

The loophole in existing law is that it affirmatively authorizes dial-a-porn for consenting adults. Thus, dial-a-porn operators are given a green light to go into business, and then the practical problem arises as to how to keep children from calling the dial-a-porn numbers . . . Moreover, there is *no good reason to authorize our interstate telephone system to be used for the communication of pornographic messages — even to adults.*" (emphasis added)

Senator Arlen Specter, speaking on an amendment to the Child Protection Act in March, 1987, gave a contrary view to that of Helms. While recognizing the need to protect children, he said,[7]

> The factual and legal issues surrounding pornography clearly are difficult and complex. Legislation in this area must be crafted carefully in light of the Constitution's protection of free speech. It is important to note that injunctions provided by this legislation do not constitute a *prior restraint of speech*. The bill makes clear that *no injunction may be issued prior to a full adversary proceeding and a final judicial determination that the material constitutes child or coerced adult pornography*." (emphasis added)

The first amendment is certainly not without limitation, indeed the Supreme Court has accepted some limit on false advertising, prayer in public schools, slander, sedition, words that threaten social harm because they advocate illegal acts, perjury, copyright violations, child porn, non-obscene sexually explicit movies shown in violation of a zoning ordinance, and indecent speech. Yet the move to include dial-a-porn was not going to be an easy one, as Specter's comment indicates.

The complexity of the Congressional debates through these years was further complicated due the fact that although there were members of Congress who were highly critical of the telephone companies, others recognized that they may have been caught in a legal bind.

There was a special concern about the companies being sued if they unilaterally cut off service.
Senator Trible addressed this concern back in 1983 when he said,[8]

> . . . This amendment requires that the defendant knowingly makes or allows to be made a communication which violates section 223 of the Communications Act. All common carriers are prohibited from listening to, or affecting the content of the telephone conversations; therefore the knowingly element will never be met by any common carrier while obeying the law and the FCC regulations.

> . . . I wish to make it perfectly clear that it is not the intent of Congress that a common carrier be prosecuted under this amendment when it is otherwise abiding by the law and the FCC regulations.

Clearly, that assurance has not led to dramatic action on the part of the companies to strike out ahead of the law. Indeed, during this period, as we shall see later, the companies were essentially waiting for legislative or regulatory action to resolve what was an increasingly difficult public relations problem for them. On the one hand, the fact that government bodies could not overcome the free speech arguments of the pornographers through either legislation or regulation supports operating company arguments that they were unable to restrict dial-a-porn. On the other hand, critics argued that there were avenues available to them, and that the companies were hiding behind the law.

In 1987, some of the operating companies began to respond to the pressure from customers and public interest groups. One measure that was introduced was that of blocking, which permitted customers to block all 976 services. Two regional companies took more aggressive measures by excluding porn producers, and were sustained in court. In 1988, Federal legislation terminated interstate dial-a-porn, pending court challenges. There are still battles going on over intrastate services.

Protect Children Against Harm

In our examination of dial-a-porn and how the telephone companies should respond to calls to eliminate it, one important ingredient is an assessment of the extent to which telephonic pornography presents a serious threat to children. Since free speech is such a basic right, strongly defended in the courts, there must be evidence of substantial harm or danger to justify a limit on any given form of expression.

A strong argument for legislative restrictions on pornography, including dial-a-porn, was presented in testimony by Alan Sears before the U. S. Senate Judiciary Committee on the Child Protection and Obscenity Enforcement Act of 1988.[9] Sears had been Executive Director of the Attorney General's Commission on Pornography in 1985 and 1986. Thus he was a very knowledgeable witness with a clear message to communicate.

Sears was testifying about pornography broadly, and dial-a-porn was only one type of pornography that he was addressing. His condemnation of pornography and the pornography industry, though, certainly apply to dial-a-porn. One of the basic points in Sears' testimony is that the content of pornography has changed dramatically since 1968, when a previous Commission had studied the subject. In a study conducted in 1985, it was found that "the most significant portion of the commercial pornography market today centers on degradation, subordination and violence."[10]

Among the findings of the studies conducted by the Commission was that the largest category of consumers of pornography in American are minors.[11] This finding ratified a similar finding in 1970 by the former Commission. Sears suggested that although the long-term impact of pornography on minors is unknown, that there may be serious consequences later in life. He said, [12]

> The total effect as to consumption by children is unknown, however, both the earlier Commission and the 1986 Commission concluded that pornography could have a serious harmful effect on the mind of a child. It was a conclusion of the 1986 Commission that pornography when exposed to young children, as it is in America today, could have a substantial impact upon the way they viewed sex, marriage, women, and the conduct of men in our society towards these important social relationships. Common sense as well as a significant body of experience confirms this proposition.

Sears' statement is important for the telephone companies on several grounds. If the studies to which he refers are correct in their assessment of the proportion of the dial-a-porn market who are minors and the potential long-term impact on male relationships with and toward women, then there is indeed a serious harm involved. Moreover, the data from 1986 studies tended to confirm material available at least sixteen years prior, which means that that information could have been available to the telephone companies.

The basic change that Sears notes is in the increase of sadomasochism, torture, rape, bestiality, and other incidents of what he sees as degradation, subordination, humiliation and victimization of women.[13] Perhaps most important for the operating companies is Sears' statement that "dial-a-porn telephonic Communications are intensely targeted toward teenagers who consume millions of dollars of this material annually."[14]

Sears concludes, on the basis of the Commission's studies, "We now know that thousands upon thousands of women have been battered and abused as a direct consequence of pornography."[15] One difficulty for our present analysis is to sort out to what extent, if at all, telephonic pornography does or could contribute to degradation or violence.

Sears gave a brief comment on the Commission's view of social science findings on the affects of pornography. The conclusion was that child pornography and pornography tied to sexual violence or degradation, submission, and humiliation all had negative affects. Again, though, there was no breakdown about types of pornography, especially with attention to any possible distinction between visual media depictions and oral messages as in dial-a-porn.

The complexity of the *fact* of harm is evidenced by Sears' citation of a recent doctoral dissertation. Sears argues that the conclusions of the dissertation support the assessment of the Commission on social science findings.[16] But a reading of the dissertation itself raises question about the type of message, visual or other, the content of the message, assertive-violent or romantic, and whether there is any impact, even with visual material, beyond the thirty minutes that was tested.[17]

Is dial-a-porn obscene or *merely* indecent? Do verbal messages have the same kind of impact that is alleged for visual messages? What is the harm that is done to a child listening to a telephonic pornographic message? There is little information on such questions. There are at least two reported cases of young boys attacking even younger girls after listening to messages, but in one case that went to court the telephone company was removed by the judge as a defendant. The lack of specific knowledge about harm, though not decisive in itself, is a very important factor for our analysis.

Sears then undertakes a Constitutional analysis of the proposed legislation in the Act. One of his major points is that the United States Supreme Court views as "compelling" the governmental interest in protecting the physical and psychological well-being of minors.[18] On Sears' view of court decisions on the matter, the proposed legislation will sustain any Constitutional challenge. This is a very important, though, unresolved issue, since FCC regulations aimed at dial-a-porn have to date been overturned.

Sears is not alone in his concerns about the harmfulness of telephonic pornography. In an attempt to support more stringent laws, Brent Ward, the U. S. Attorney for Utah testified in 1986 before a House committee considering legislation specifically dealing with dial-a-porn. Ward was at that time the only U. S. Attorney who had successfully prosecuted a dial-a-porn company, which he saw as evidence of inadequate legislation. For our purposes, the inability of law enforcement to stop dial-a-porn could be used to argue that the companies, lacking the power of the law, would be less able to do anything. A contrary argument can be made that business firms might have alternative ways to act when legal agencies had their hands tied. We need to examine this more fully later.

In response to what he described as hundreds of complaints from parents whose 10 to 16 year old children had called a New York number, Ward brought in an indictment. In Wards words, [19]

> The indictment charged that in response to the children's calls Carlin transmitted explicit, recorded dramatizations of sex acts alleged to be obscene, including sodomy, rape, incest, bestiality, sadomasochism and excretory eroticism. Most of the children had made many calls. One boy had made more that 700 calls.

In his testimony, Ward dealt with the psychological damage that dial-a-porn can do. Whereas Sears dealt with pornography more broadly and did not separate visual and oral messages, Ward turned to an expert on the effects of obscenity who focused on telephonic messages. In the view of Victor Cline, a psychologist, the verbal messages tended to socialize in an unhealthy way and excessive exposure can become a "time bomb" in the life of a child. Although adults might scoff at the material, children are likely to color future sexual attitudes, thinking, and conduct. As Ward put it, [20]

> He concluded these messages had a powerful addictive effect that had adversely influenced the behavior of the children. These listening experiences became vivid memories which the

mind continually replayed, thus stimulating the child again and again and suggested the need to make more calls. Dr. Cline found that exposure to these messages tended to condition the children to associate sexual arousal with the abuse and degradation of women and with violence and pain.

Cline was writing in 1984 when protests against telephonic messages were being made in substantial number. Is there a burden on a business firm to search for and evaluate this kind of information when faced with a challenge of the kind presented by dial-a-porn? Is the burden on the company to terminate the problem if there is evidence of harm or is that responsibility properly that of parents or legal agencies?

As Ward indicated, parents expressed frustration about controlling access to this form of pornography. The telephone as a means of communication was all-pervasive, and parents cannot monitor their children at home and elsewhere at all times.

Ward was also frustrated, at least in part, in his legal efforts. He lost the case against Carlin Communications when the case was dismissed because the law could only be enforced against the "calling" party. Carlin was the "called" party since someone would have to dial their number to initiate the call. The judge also said that messages are not "matter" that can be "transported" within the meaning of the applicable statutes. A Court of Appeals justice talked about "traffic in verbal sewage," but affirmed the dismissal under existing law and called upon Congress to act.[21]

Ward makes the point that others had previously made that the 1983 legislation in response to dial-a-porn had resulted in legalizing obscenity. That was done by providing a complete defense to providers if they can demonstrate compliance with the FCC access code rule. The practical effect is to permit the dissemination of obscene dial-a-porn. This is something which in his judgment goes against a number of Supreme Court decisions, beginning with *Miller v. California*, the 1973 decision that established the obscenity definition.

Ward did win a case that was brought against another company called Adult Entertainment Network Inc., but it was not because of any change in law. Rather, the head of the company wanted to avoid adverse publicity and agreed to pay a $100,000 fine and to discontinue its dial-a-porn service in all twelve cities.

Ward, then, supported the idea that telephonic pornography is harmful to children, and he also argued strongly that existing law was inadequate to protect children from harm. Given the situation, he argues for stronger laws, but he also suggests that the telephone companies have legal options open to them. We will consider those suggestions when we look at types of telephone company responses later on.

Preservation of Free Speech

Protection of children against harm comes up squarely against the preservation of free speech, and, as we have seen, the free speech consideration has taken precedence so far in the dial-a-porn conflict. In the midst of growing public concern and protests over dial-a-porn, the case for free speech was made by Barry Lynn, an attorney for the ACLU, in testimony in September 1987 before a House subcommittee considering regulation of telephone communication. Lynn's basic position was stated as follows,[22]

> We believe that regulation of the content of individual or commercial telephone communications beyond that in current law raises grave First Amendment problems regarding censorship and personal privacy.

He went on to point out that current law already prohibits obscene or indecent communications to persons under the age of eighteen or to adults who do not wish to hear such communications.

The ACLU was particularly concerned that the 1987 legislation, HR 1786, would make transmission of obscene or indecent materials over the telephone a federal crime *even to consenting adults*. The proposed legislation would also remove a possible defense by porn providers to prosecution if they would take specific steps to prevent access of minors to sexually-oriented telephone services.

The consenting adult concern is especially important for our discussion because embedded in it are several of the ethical considerations which make dial-a-porn so complex.

• The central concern for adults, of course, is privacy. There is a long history of litigation and Supreme Court decisions that relate to a competent, consenting adult reading and viewing what he or she wishes in the privacy of the home.

• The other side of the privacy issue, of course, is freedom of speech — or free expression. In order for privacy to have any significance for users of pornography (or politically sensitive material) someone has to be able to produce and distribute it.

The ACLU's Lynn put it simply, "H. R. 1786 (the proposed legislation) is constitutionally unacceptable in that it violates rights of privacy and free expression, and is unconstitutionally vague and overbroad."[23]

For the ACLU, a "high-water mark" in Supreme Court decisions on sexually-oriented materials and privacy came in 1969 when the Court overruled a state law that would penalize the mere possession of obscene material. That decision though has been eroded by later rulings that permitted prohibition of the receipt of magazines through the mail and importation of obscene films, even though the material was intended for private use.

The erosion of the strict privacy standard clearly concerns the ACLU, and they don't want to see it further eroded. They are also concerned that the existing limitations could be applied to telephone communications. Accordingly, they want to set telephone communications apart. Lynn says,[24]

> . . . material by telephone is different from receipt of the material through bookstores, theaters, and the United States Postal Service, and should be protected.

Is telephone communication different in kind? What Lynn argues is that the highly private nature of telephone communication sets it apart. He points out that there is legislation requiring search warrants for wiretapping and case law that protects the privacy of the person who "pays the toll."

He goes on to say,[25]

> ... Voluntary use of "Dial-a-Porn" intrudes upon no privacy rights of others, and there are no unwilling participants. The service can be accessed only by the affirmative act of a voluntary participant who has clear knowledge of what he or she is about to hear and experience. It is a quintessential example of the right of individuals privately to receive information and ideas.

I agree that it is indeed a fine example on which to argue for privacy, although I am not certain that the mail carrier, cable TV technician, or video store rental clerk is a very involved third party. It seems to me that a strong case can be made that dial-a-porn messages are similar to things received through the mail or on cable TV as far as the access of children.

Current Federal law says that "dissemination by telephone of any obscene or indecent communication to persons under eighteen years of age is unlawful." What Lynn is arguing against in 1987 is the extension of the law to make unlawful the commercial transmission of "indecent" messages to adults by outlawing all such communication. The ACLU, in effect, is trying to hold the line on limits established through a number of Supreme Court cases and insure that privacy is not further eroded.[26]

Lynn, of course, is not alone in arguing for the protection of free speech against limitation, despite an obviously good cause. Recall, for example, Senator Specter's strong statement against legislation that would constitute prior restraint in the debate over the Child Protection Act in 1987. And, as we have seen, the courts have consistently ruled in favor of free speech over aggressive limitation of dial-a-porn even though it was seen as "verbal sewage."

What Lynn has not addressed so far, regardless of the importance of his argument in protection of privacy, is the matter of protecting children. Lynn is obviously aware of that. Is the ACLU arguing for access by minors to Dial-a-porn? Obviously not. In order to argue for privacy rights of adults and an absolute ban on dial-a-porn, Lynn sets forth several alternative proposals. All of the proposals depend upon enhancing parental supervision of communication technologies in the home. It is, after all, the responsibility of parents to exercise all sorts of control over material that is potentially harmful to their children.

Lynn makes a number of proposals for limiting access to telephonic pornography that do not require new legislation and, therefore, do not imperil free speech. One suggestion that he makes is for the telephone companies to engage in what is called "blocking," a procedure that would cut off all 976 services to subscribers. He argues that such an approach is Constitutional because it is content and viewpoint neutral.[27] The telephone companies oppose such an approach because they would lose revenue from a variety of profitable 976 services.

An alternative to company initiated blocking is through placing blocking equipment in individual homes, although, again, all 976 services would be cut off. Various blocking approaches might also impose a cost to consumers from a few dollars up to $100. Lynn argues that it is appropriate for parents to pay "since the burden of controlling children's exposure to sexually

oriented materials (as with any materials) must ultimately rest with parents."[28]

Another suggestion that Lynn makes includes message scrambling. Adult customers desiring to receive
messages would have to purchase descrambling devices.
Although the cost to the consumers would be modest,
both the providers and phone companies would likely
be opposed because this requires action on the part of
the customer significantly beyond just dialing the phone
and the bother and time might reduce business. Indeed,
since customer premises blocking equipment is available, the ACLU favors that approach over scrambling
precisely because the latter imposes an impediment to
adults who spontaneously wish to hear dial-it messages.

Still another approach that Lynn reviews is the use of
an access code or credit card number to identify legitimate users. Although feasible, Lynn expresses a concern over the heavy financial burden to sexually oriented dial-a-service providers. Even more worrisome to
the ACLU is that this approach would require keeping
computerized records of adults who have codes. As
Lynn says, "This would raise serious privacy concerns,
and the risk of possible disclosure would be likely to
deter potential users, thus having a chilling effect on the
industry."[29]

The ACLU is in favor of limiting access of minors to
telephonic pornography. It is clear, though, from the
last quoted statement that the ACLU wants to protect
both the free speech rights of providers and the privacy
rights of adults who choose to listen to pornography.
The ACLU position needs to be seen in its consistent
attempts to resist limitations on any kind of unpopular

or controversial speech, whether that involves sex or politics.[30]

The Response of the Phone Companies

Dial-a-Porn has been a mixed blessing for the telephone companies — trying, frustrating, distasteful on the one hand, quite profitable on the other. For example, in the most recently reported year, the total revenue from all 976 service calls, including sports, weather, finance, etc. to all telephone companies in California was $70 million, and of that about 60 per cent of the revenue came from Dial-a-Porn. Pacific Bell alone made at least $12 million from Dial-a-Porn in a recent year.

The phone companies maintain that they have wanted to eliminate dial-a-porn from the outset of 976 services, that it is distasteful, and that they have been blocked from acting because of their common carrier status. As we shall see, the picture is much more complicated than that, and there is suspicion that the expressed distaste was outweighed by the sizeable profits to be earned by continuing the service. As pressure on the companies has mounted and the potential damage to reputation has increased, there has been some change in the response and action of the companies.

Thus far, a full picture of the development of strategy and positions within the companies is not available, but testimony before Congressional committees and public relations statements provide some insight into their thinking.

Among the major positions taken by the phone companies are the following:

(1) We are Common Carriers

As regulated utilities with a monopoly in their designated service area, the telephone companies are required to offer service to all qualified applicants on a non-discriminatory basis. The companies are officially known as "common carriers." One example of the use of this role to make an argument against independent action is that of NYNEX, the parent corporation of New York Telephone, in response to being criticized for taking a "neutral" stance on dial-a-porn. In an April, 1986, letter to the Attorney General's Commission on Pornography, a NYNEX official said,[31]

> . . . as common carriers, we have a statutory obligation to make our services available to all members of the public without discrimination. We cannot deny service to any customer on the basis of our own disapproval or public outcry.

In October of the same year, Pacific Bell issued a media release with a set of questions and answers. The first question that they posed was, "WHAT IS YOUR POSITION REGARDING '976' DIAL-A-PORN SERVICES?" In response, they began by saying,[32]

> . . . We do not like the fact that dial-a-porn is available over "976." We are most concerned that it is available to children.
> . . .

The release then went on, though, to say

> However, after studying all our options, we have decided at this time that our obligation as a common carrier outweighs the desire to try to unilaterally disconnect providers of sexually explicit messages.

They move later in the release to talk about some protection that can be offered to customers to control access, but in the balance of things their common carrier status takes precedence.

How real, or how substantial, is the common carrier "defense" against doing nothing? Does the common carrier status block the companies from independent action to terminate dial-a-porn? The picture is mixed, as noted below:

• In 1983, the California Public Utilities Commission (CPUC) did in fact refuse a proposed "tariff" (a plan to provide services) from Pac Bell that would have permitted refusal of 976 lines to dial-a-porn providers. Pac Bell has used the CPUC action to argue that their capacity to act unilaterally was weakened by the CPUC. A former staff member of the CPUC said that although the tariff was indeed refused, that Pac Bell was told that they could act on their own as a business and did not need CPUC authority to withhold the 976 lines from the porn producers.

• Pacific Bell's appeal to the obligation of the common carrier is somewhat strange in view of its actions and attempted actions in court from 1983 to 1987. In 1983 it told one provider that it would seek a court order to disconnect its service if the provider offered dial-a-porn in California. A year later, though, after legal maneuvering, a Federal court judge denied Pacific's request for an order to disconnect service because such an order would be prior restraint in violation of the First Amendment. The judge reiterated this position in a decision involving another provider in 1987.[33] Yet, even before that decision, Pac Bell had released its Media Press Release with the common carrier statement.

• When Mountain Bell, under some pressure from the State of Arizona, moved to terminate access to 976 by dial-a-porn producers, a Federal Court supported their action despite the common carrier status. The Court said, in part, that Mountain Bell did not need to enter into any business that in its judgment was going to hurt its reputation. The Court also said that as far as 976 was concerned, whatever Mountain Bell did would not be considered state action, and thus subject to common carrier regulation, in contrast to its basic residential and commercial telephone services.

Although it is not certain that other operating companies would have won a case on the same grounds in other jurisdictions, given judicial history regarding dial-a-porn, Southern Bell did win judicial support for withholding service to some providers on grounds of danger to reputation. Yet, not all have attempted to pursue this line, even though it was successful in at least two jurisdictions. Pacific Bell, for example, declined to pursue this legal avenue to restrict dial-a-porn despite its success elsewhere.

(2) We Are Not Police, Nor Public Censors

A second argument that the NYNEX spokesman put forward in writing to the Attorney General's Pornography Commission fits very well with one of Milton Friedman's set of reasons as to why corporations and corporate executives should not try to determine public policy. The NYNEX representative said,[34]

> Moreover, we are telephone companies, not policemen. We are not qualified to act in the role of public censor, nor are we willing to assume the risk of doing so.

This particular argument raises a fundamental question not only for the present discussion regarding dial-a-porn but for the social responsibility of business firms. Similar questions come up on other issues, most notably South Africa, affirmative action, and the environment. The position that one takes on these issues may reflect a basic philosophical position on the role of business firms or it may be based on the seriousness of the perceived harm and the impact that any action would have.

(3) We Will Follow the Law

One of the important questions regarding appropriate action by a a business firm is what kind of leadership position it should take when there is a social problem related to its business that is not being addressed. The options vary quite a bit, but they boil down to deciding to take decisive action beyond what is required by law or to wait until there is a legal requirement (along with legal protection) for taking some action. The significance of the lead/no lead question looms larger in the context of the NYNEX representative's statement that reads,[35]

> Any time an appropriate law enforcement agency establishes that one of our customers is using our service in an unlawful manner, we can and we will promptly terminate service to

that customer. As yet, no such showing has been made with respect to Dial-a-Porn.

This response, of course, goes to the heart of our discussion in that the companies are saying that they will obey the law, but that what is legal is established elsewhere.

We can find both support and problems with that view when we look at the complicated picture of the Congress, the Courts, and the FCC at the national level and State and federal Legislative bodies. On the one hand, they had clear responsibility for setting and enforcing the standards, protecting children and penalizing violators. On the other hand, for over five years they have been largely ineffective in their efforts to monitor and control the situation. If effective alternatives were available to the telephone companies under existing law, their level of responsibility may have increased.

One forceful argument for companies taking the lead was made by U. S. Attorney Brent Ward in his aforementioned testimony during 1987 House hearings. In talking about his activities in working with Mountain Bell in a suit against a carrier, he spoke of his skepticism over the telephone companies' position that their common carrier status prevents them from terminating a provider on the basis of the content of the message. He was bolstered by the Mountain Bell decision to terminate dial-a-porn services, an action upheld recently by the U. S. Court of Appeals for the 9th circuit[36] and success in court by Southern Bell.[37] Ward's question was if these two companies could succeed in court on grounds of protecting their reputation, why could not the others? He said,[38]

> But, beyond any action you may take there is also action some telephone companies have already taken that other telephone companies should perhaps consider taking. This action consists of a contractual requirement altogether barring sexual content from mass announcement or dial-it lines.

He goes ahead to describe what Mountain Bell did in Utah. It developed a *Guide for 976 Message Providers*, with one heading being "Sexual Content Prohibited." The Guideline specified a range of things that could not be said or suggested, and then said,[39]

> . . . if Mountain Bell finds that the message or program offered by the sponsor over the Scoopline Service (their 976) violates the foregoing standard (which shall be determined in the sole opinion of Mountain Bell, reasonably applying the foregoing standard), then this contract and/or the service provided hereby may be immediately terminated by Mountain Bell . . . without further liability. Any determination made by Mountain Bell that the sponsor has violated the foregoing standard shall not be subject to challenge or appeal in any forum by the sponsor in the absence of bad faith, fraud, malice or gross negligence on the part of Mountain Bell.

In the Southern Bell case it was decided that the company could deny access to subscribers whose messages might tarnish its "corporate image." The court ruled that a private business is free to choose the content of messages with which its name and reputation will be associated and that such a choice is not the exercise of a public function. Ward called on other companies to follow their lead.[40]

On the one hand, Ward does suggest a legally feasible plan for company initiated efforts to deal with the dial-a-porn problem. On the other hand, the Mountain Bell guideline raises serious questions about the exercise of this kind of authority. The lack of any recourse or form of due process to which the provider must agree clearly challenges free speech concerns and on its face appears to be a blatant form of prior restraint. One might support the effort to protect corporate reputation as a tactic without endorsing the Mountain Bell language.

The above discussion helps to focus our basic theme of beyond compliance. NYNEX is using the current state of the law as a basis to say that nothing can be done. Ward is arguing that the operating companies can successfully challenge the producers of telephonic pornography through aggressive use of the law. NYNEX argued that since neither Congress nor the FCC have been able to come up with a workable solution, ". . . our 'neutrality' is nothing more, and nothing less, than what is required of us. We have not found, nor has anyone suggested, any other viable course of action for a telephone company to take."[41]

That statement focuses our discussion in an interesting and important way. In *Resort Properties*, ICI, the selling company, was faced with a decision that would be made totally out of the public eye and a problem that was not the focus of legal activity on all sides. ICI's problem was what it *should* do, in the face of established law, beyond the law. With Dial-a-Porn, the question is what, if anything, a company can or should do when law making and law enforcement agencies cannot or will not address the problem. Certainly the distinction here must affect our final assessment of the responsibility that the companies have.

(4) Maintaining Dial-a-Porn is Profitable

Critics have maintained that the reason that companies have not taken action to stop dial-a-porn on their own is that they don't want to give up the profits.

It is very difficult to find a bald statement to that effect by an operating company, but I have talked with employees from several operating companies who have suggested that the policy of their company has been driven as much by profit as by having their hands legally tied.

One example of a written statement, and one that was crafted by the public relations department of one of the baby bells, is a response to its own hypothetical question. This was in late 1987 right after Mountain Bell had won the right in court to terminate dial-a-porn services. The exchange went as follows: [42]

WHY DOESN'T THE RECENT COURT DECISION INVOLVING MOUNTAIN BELL GIVE YOU THE RIGHT TO REFUSE "976" SERVICE TO DIAL-A-PORN PROVIDERS?

The response was that the long process of taking this matter to court would "not be in the best interests of the company or its shareholders."

That statement is ambiguous and could refer to legal costs as well as to the unstated matter of continuing a profitable venture. That it might be the latter is reinforced by the subsequent Question and Answer in the media release, which read: [43]

DOES THAT MEAN YOU ARE GIVING UP THE
FIGHT TO REMOVE DIAL-A-PORN FROM THE
NETWORK?

Even though we are still unhappy with having dial-a-porn on
the network, we are not going to remove it unilaterally.

There is no further explanation of what that statement means. It simply goes on to begin detailing safe-
guards that it will introduce, including educational
material on 976 to parents and children and the intro-
duction of blocking.

The message that the media release sends in its Q and
A structure is interesting, especially since Mountain Bell
had recently won the right to exclude "adult messages."
In the same release, Pac Bell says that it opposed
pornography in their original 976 tariff and that it is still
unhappy with having dial-a-porn on its network. Yet,
provided with a legal precedent from a U.S. Appeals
Court, it chooses not to act "unilaterally."

Why? Why else than that the cost, in legal fees and
lost revenue, is too high?

There is similar ambiguity and question raised in
NYNEX testimony before a House committee in
September of 1987. The representative said, "NYNEX
finds 'dial-a-porn' repugnant, is unalterably opposed to
it and applauds the Congressional interest in seeking a
constitutional way to end it." He went on, though, to
raise again the rejection of the censorship role and
being legally liable for denial of transmission to any
porn providers. Then, in a phrase reflective of the Pac
Bell press release (issued one month later), the
NYNEX representative said, ". . . But until the state of

the law is settled, NYNEX does not believe that it should today refuse to carry 'dial-a-porn.' "[44]

The legal picture, as mentioned earlier, is complex, and indeed the FCC had proposed regulations overturned in court, but the refusal to act until the law is settled, despite the expressed repugnance with dial-a-porn, raises questions about the commitment to exclude or terminate the service.

One could argue that it is *precisely because* no satisfactory legal remedy has been found that the operating companies should act.

What Could the Companies Have Done?

There are a range of actions that the companies could have taken. Some of the actions would have involved risk of legal exposure; some others have actually been taken, but only recently and somewhat reluctantly; and still others would have required an imaginative type of leadership not seen thus far. The possible options include:

1. refuse service to dial-a-porn, risk a lawsuit

2. terminate dial-a-porn, risk a lawsuit

3. introduce blocking much earlier
   also look at other options, e. g. screening and scrambling

4. introduce special 900 channel for adult entertainment much earlier

5. terminate all 976

   this has been a legally available option all along, but it was also a costly one in that significant revenues would be lost.

6. take the lead in pushing for legislation and regulation through lobbying efforts.

7. undertake an advertising and mass media campaign to protect its reputation and garner support for restrictions.

8. refuse to keep revenue and/or profit from the mandated provision of 976 lines to porn producers.

9. introduce the interactive, credit card number requirement at an earlier date.

10. undertake review of available data and studies on pornography to determining if it does or does not have the potential for serious and long-lasting harmful effects on minors.

Conclusion

The dial-a-porn case that was posed at the outset of this lecture provides an excellent example of the kind of ethical issues that business firms may face. Because of the larger context of government agencies involved, it is ideal for examination of the extent to which business firms can turn to the law as the definer of ethical guidelines.

The conflicting positions represented by advocates of tighter controls on behalf of protecting children and advocates for protecting privacy and free speech add significantly to the complexity of the situation—and to the problem that the operating companies had in deciding how to respond. Indeed, this is precisely the kind of issue that focuses the debate about the social responsibility of businesses and whether they can or should be moral agents.

There were clear ethical issues that the operating companies had to acknowledge and face. The basic, and most important ethical issue, is that of the protection of children against harm vs. the protection of privacy (adult consumers) and free speech (porn producers). A second issue, more directly applicable to the telephone companies, is that of the legitimate pursuit of profit over against protection of children from potential harm.

In the context of the total environment—the business, political, social, and legal realities—though, the ethical issues tended to become somewhat obscured. It was left primarily to public interest groups on each side, along with Senators and Members of Congress, to clearly enunciate the basic interests to be protected or preserved. From the public testimony and documents that were available, the telephone company representatives shaped their responses very much in terms of their role as common carriers. Pacific Bell took some early litigation initiatives, but then seemed to retreat to the common carrier defense. Other operating companies took action to terminate service when their reputations suffered or, as in one reported instance, law enforcement pressured aggressive action. There is not an overall pattern, though, of movement to protect the public interest against a potentially harmful product.

The whole concept of "common carrier," of course, is one that denotes neutrality and non-censoriousness. That, coupled with the very strong tradition we have toward protecting free speech from arbitrary restraint and control, provides not only an explanation but some support for the posture that the companies adopted. We would expect and want the telephone companies to provide access to its service on an impartial, non-discriminatory basis. Such equal access for all kinds of speech is a public good.

The question that the dial-a-porn case raises for the operating companies, though, is whether in such circumstances, with public outcry, impassioned speeches by Senators and Members of Congress, and some evidence of psychological harm to children, they can continue to remain neutral, to be merely common carriers. Should the companies have taken steps beyond appeal to regulators, legislators, and the courts to restrict dial-a-porn? Was there something about the situation which required that the normal, socially defined role was not sufficient? My answer is in the affirmative.

I contend that the *possibility* that dial-a-porn was severely harmful to minors created a situation that required that the companies step out of, or transcend, the common carrier role and consider alternative courses of action. The common carrier role is indeed neutral, and the initial effort to seek regulatory and legislative warrant to limit dial-a-porn was wholly in character and legitimate. When those efforts failed, though, the companies were then challenged to consider whether there was a sufficient reason to cease neutrality and become proactive.

Suggesting that the companies should have been more forthcoming and assertive is not to conclude that, finally, they should have terminated access by porn producers to the telephone lines. The case for privacy and free speech made by Lynn of the ACLU is important and persuasive. The limitation on due process in the policy adopted by Mountain Bell is chilling. Yet, in my judgment, the ultimate decision on whether dial-a-porn should be limited must be based on whether or not such communications do in fact cause harm to minors. The fact that the messages are distasteful to some people is not sufficient to warrant termination as long as the messages do not fall within that which is defined as obscene. Modes of limiting access to minors short of termination is possible, as indicated at the end of the preceding section. The competing interests need to be weighed carefully in making a final decision.

One thing that the case and our analysis of the situation reveals for the larger discussion of the action of business firms beyond what the law requires relates to changes that occur over time. Before 1983, the problem of telephonic pornography did not exist because the phone companies controlled the content of 976 services. In 1983, and the year or two following, when the problem emerged and expanded in scope, it was only natural that the companies would turn to the regulators, the legislators, and the courts to deal with a distasteful problem. This is not to say that the companies did not have a problem; rather, it is to recognize that especially in a highly regulated industry that the first response to a problem is to move to process, to structure. By 1984 or 1985, though, it became apparent that there was not going to be a quick and effective legal solution.

I contend that as the inability of the legal agencies to respond effectively, at least in the short run, became more apparent, the burden on the companies to take some action increased. As we have seen, there were a number of possible things that the companies could have done. Some of the responses would have been more risky in terms of legal exposure; some of the responses would have been more costly financially; and some of the responses would have required a kind of proactive leadership role *vis-s-vis* a social issue than was customary for the telephone companies.

The record that is available in the form of public statements and published testimony, indicates that the companies, at best, took a passive role in the face of growing complaints about dial-a-porn. They expressed their distaste for the content of dial-a-porn and regret that such material was communicated over their lines, but were loath to take any of a variety of possible actions. Even when two of the operating companies were sustained in Federal courts when they did act to restrict telephonic pornography, the two largest regional companies declined to follow suit.

To be sure, each of the possible actions available to the companies, short of new legislation, would be costly in terms of lost present business or possible loss of future business. Yet, the companies had been and were receiving substantial revenue from the very service that they decried. That alone might have argued for early adoption of blocking and other measures which were only initiated in late 1987.

Although a full analysis of the effects of pornography is far beyond the scope of the present analysis, there is a growing body of literature, some of which is cited earlier, that suggests that telephonic pornography may be harmful to children. In my judgment, the potential for harm warranted action by the companies to restrict the communication of telephonic pornography until the question of harm is resolved. Any one of several suggested possible actions could have accomplished at least temporary limitation of dial-a-porn. Unilateral termination of the service might have ultimately lost in the courts and would have been expensive, but it would have bought time. Suspension of all 976 services would have been costly, but it would have certainly prevented potential harm. One of these actions, or others, coupled with encouragement of more certain determination of potential harm to minors, possibly through funding studies, would have been a more forceful and appropriate response than the pattern reviewed earlier. In fact, the companies tended to tut-tut but take refuge behind the legal agencies. Such a response, in the face of potential serious harm, was not sufficient.

Ethical issues often demand moral imagination for their resolution. The resolution often calls for aggressive action beyond compliance with the law.

Notes

1. NYNEX letter, April 9, 1986.

2. *Congressional Record*, March 25, 1987, E1123.

3. 47 U. S. C. Section 223 (b) (I) (A).

4. *Congressional Record — Senate*, S16796, December 1, 1987.

5. *Congressional Record*, E1123, March 15, 1987.

6. *Congressional Record — Senate*, S438, January 6, 1987.

7. *Congressional Record — Senate*, S2932, March 10, 1987.

8. *Congressional Record — Senate*, S16867, November 18, 1983.

9. Statement of Alan E. Sears, Legal Counsel, Citizens for Decency through Law, U. S. Senate Judiciary Committee, June 8, 1988, On S. 2033, Child Protection and Obscenity Enforcement Act of 1988.

10. *Ibid.*, p. 5.

11. *Ibid.*, p. 6.

12. *Ibid.*, p. 6.

13. *Ibid.*, p. 5.

14. *Ibid.*, p. 7.

15. *Ibid.*, p. 15.

16. *Ibid.*, p. 12.

17. *Ibid.*, Exhibit B, Weaver, James, *Effects of Portrayals of Female Sexuality and Violence Against Women on Perceptions of Women*, unpublished dissertation, Indiana Univ., 1987.

18. *Ibid.*, p. 17.

19. Ward, Brent D., Testimony before the Committee on Energy and Commerce Subcommittee on Telecommunications and Finance, U. S. House of Representatives, Sept. 30, 1986, p. 2.

20. *Ibid.*, p. 2.

21. *Ibid.*, p. 4 citing *United States v. Carlin Communications, Inc.*, No. 85-CR-86J (D. Utah, decided September 30, 1985); aff'd 815 F.2d 1367 (10th Cir. 1987).

22. Lynn, Barry, Testimony before the Telecommunications and Finance Subcommittee of the House Energy and Commerce Committee, Sept., 1987, p. 2.

23. *Ibid.*, p. 3.

24. *Ibid.*, p. 4.

25. *Ibid.*, p. 5.

26. *Ibid.*, p. 7.

27. *Ibid.*, p. 12.

28. *Ibid.*, p. 15.

29. *Ibid.*, p. 18.

30. *Ibid.*, p. 18.

31. Letter from Ivan Seidenberg, NYNEX, to Alan E. Sears, Exec. Dir., Attorney General's Commission for Pornography, April 9, 1986, p. 2.

32. Pacific Bell Media Press Release, 10/14/87, p. 5.

33. Pacific Bell internal communication summarizing litigation on 976 programs from Sept. 1983 to Oct. 1988. It is not clear if the successive losses in court discouraged further judicial action on the part of Pacific Bell or if another case already in litigation negated additional lawsuits at this time. In any event, the "obligation as a common carrier" statement in November, 1987, signaled a passive stance pending regulatory or legislative action.

34. Seidenberg letter, *op. cit.*, p. 2.

35. *Ibid.*, p. 2.

36. *Carlin Communications, Inc. v. Mountain States Telephone and Telegraph Company*, No. 85-2797 (9th Cir., decided Sept. 14, 1987).

37. *Carlin Communications, Inc. v. Southern Bell Telephone & Telegraph Co.*, 802 F.2d 1352 (11th Cir. 1986).

38. Ward, *op. cit.*, p. 11.

39. *Ibid.*, pp. 11-12.

40. *Ibid.*, p. 12.

41. Seidenberg letter, *op. cit.*, p. 2.

42. Pacific Bell Media Press Release, *op. cit.*

43. *Ibid.*

44. Statement of Robert H. Helgeson, NYNEX, before House Committee on Energy and Commerce, Subcommittee on Telecommunications and Finance, hearing on HR 1786, The Telephone Decency Act, Sept. 30, 1987.

Lecture 3

The Meaning of Integrity: The Use of Proprietary Information

About two months ago I was conducting one of a series of four hour seminars on ethics for a local firm. During a period when the participants were divided into small groups doing case analysis, I moved from group to group. In one break-out room there was a large black board—pasted on it in very large letters was a slogan:

At the left side, the two words WIN ETHICALLY
On the right side, the two words BUT WIN

The slogan was representative or symbolic of the place of ethics in many businesses.

The obvious problem that arises for managers and firms is that in highly competitive markets, with short decision times and high stakes for each contract or sale won or lost, winning often puts pressure on, or competes with, that action which might be considered ethical.

This is the third in the series of lectures that bear the overall title of Beyond Compliance. I have chosen that theme because in work that I have done with a number of large firms, in many different industries, I find that the understanding of ethics is too often constrained to that which is defined by law.

As a basic question to frame all three lectures, I have taken a question posed by Alan Goodman. He says, [1]

> The question is not whether people in business should observe legal limits, but whether they ought to recognize moral obligations beyond the requirements of law, when assumption of such obligations is incompatible with maximization of profit. Should managers sacrifice profits for moral reasons not incorporated in law, or can they assume that pursuit of profit within legal limits will tend toward a more moral outcome?

For example, I would argue that Johnson and Johnson answered Goldman's question in the affirmative in the Tylenol case; whereas when Ford considered its design decisions on the fuel integrity system of the Pinto it answered negatively.

We may put these three lectures into three theoretical "locations": first, the corporate social responsibility debate of the 1970's; second, the moral agency debate of the 1980's; and third, my understanding of the relation of law and ethics. Law defines what we are permitted to do, required to do, or prohibited from doing; ethics concerns what we ought to do or should do.

The fact that something is lawful doesn't mean that the ethical question has been resolved for each person or organization, but it does provide a clear signal to everyone as to what is generally acceptable.

Some examples of the application of law in the three suggested modes are:

Permission: *Roe v Wade*, the decision on abortion in 1973, established abortion on demand in the first trimester as the law of the land in all 50 states—abortion was permissible. The decision did not remove the moral or ethical question for individual women or couples, nor for health professionals of particular religious persuasions or some hospitals run by churches or religious orders.

Requirement: Most states require disclosure of a defect or potential problem on improved property, but, as we saw in our discussion of *Resort Properties* in Lecture One, not all states require disclosure on unimproved property. The ethical dilemma that faced ICI and Joe Straightshooter was whether they should disclose a potential flooding problem in the absence of a legal requirement.

Prohibition: The law prohibits the transmission of obscene messages over the telephone. Nonetheless, the courts will not issue injunctions against potentially obscene messages on the grounds that that would constitute prior restraint. Thus, as we saw in Lecture Two, the telephone companies were faced with the question of whether they should push for new legislation or take independent action, at some cost, to restrict dial-a-porn.

In a sense, we can say that the law defines the moral minimum.

Here is a case to help frame our discussion.

Just a Little Help

You are the senior manager in your firm responsible for marketing a new computerized telecommunications system to the Federal government. Competition is very stiff, and the company that obtains the initial contract will be very likely to receive additional business on the system for years to come. Your superior has made it very clear that obtaining this contract would be a major breakthrough for the company—and for you. Your company has been doing well, but it needs to position itself for marketing new technology in the years to come.

You know that there are several other firms that are developing similar systems to yours and that bidding will be very tough. Negotiations with the Federal agency that wants the product has given you clear knowledge of agency needs and a fairly clear idea of the ballpark purchasing price. Undoubtedly your competitors have similar information.

One week before you are to submit your final bid, a member of your staff comes to your office in a very excited state. He puts a large file on your desk and smiles broadly as you open the file and see that you are holding a copy of the final bid of your major competitor. Under close questioning it becomes clear that the information has come into your agent's hands from a disgruntled Federal employee. Your staff member assures you that he did not pay anything for the bid nor make any explicit promises of reward in exchange for the competitor's bid.

If the use of the bid under these conditions is illegal, then you have to decide whether you will skirt or violate the law.

So assume that the law on use of bids under the conditions outlined is blurry—you did not pay anything for the information. It is also the case in many industries that all kinds of information and misinformation is floating around in situations of this type.

What would you do?

In the real situation on which the case is based, the company decided to use the information and secured a large government contract. A major competitor "smelled" something in the awarding of the contract and demanded, as was its right, to see figures on the winning bid. When it discovered close parallels to its own bid, with appropriate downward adjustments, the competitor threatened to sue. The company in the case gave up its contract, choosing not to go through litigation, and the ultimate award went to the competitor.

Of some interest to our discussion is the fact that in every instance in which I have used *Just a little Help* in seminars with business firms, the overwhelming, almost unanimous, response is to refuse to use the competitor's bid and to notify the contracting agency that the bid process has been compromised. Yet, in the real situation, the company used the information.

Now consider the following possible use of competitor information:

Where do you Draw the Line?

You are on a flight and cannot help but overhear two competitor personnel sitting together in the row ahead of you. You know who they are, but you are sure that they do not know who you are. They are talking about a program on which they are bidding - the same bid on which you are working for your firm.

Check your response on each of the following possibilities:

	Yes	No
• Is it okay for you to actively listen to what they are saying with a view toward picking up useful information?	____	____
• Their conversation continues with a lot of numbers being mentioned. Is it okay for you to take a few notes?	____	____
• The material is coming faster than you can write. Would it be okay to turn on your dictating machine and hold it where it will pick up the conversation?	____	____
• As your competitors disembark from the plane, you see that they have left some materials in the seat-back pocket. Do you take them?	____	____
• The material are NOT marked confidential or classified. Is it okay to use them?	____	____
• The material ARE marked confidential. Is okay for you to use them?	____	____
• When you get into your hotel, you see your competitors at the check-in desk. Is it okay for you to frequent the hotel bar to see if you can pick up more information?	____	____
• You find to your surprise that you are placed in the room next to your competitors. Is it okay to turn down your TV in order to hear what they are saying?	____	____
• Even with the TV turned off, the voices are muffled. Is it okay to put your ear to the wall to hear better?	____	____
• If the voices are still not clear, is it okay to put a drinking glass against the wall to enhance their voices?	____	____

Whatever pattern of responses you made to various choices presented in *WHERE DO YOU DRAW THE LINE?*, the responses of people in business, in several different industries, is instructive. The great majority, for example, think that it is alright to actively listen on the airplane. The basic rationale here is that people shouldn't talk in public about matters which should be confidential; therefore it is not a violation of any ethical norm to listen and take advantage of what is being said. (There is also a cynical view which suggests that you are recognized and disinformation is being deliberately communicated.) The responses grow varied, though, when people move down the list. A fair number of people think that it is alright to take notes but not to use a dictating machine. There are also some interesting (and amusing) discussions about the difference between putting one's ear to the wall and using a drinking glass to enhance voices.

There are two important points to make in regard to the pattern of responses: first, since all of the items on the list deal with the use of competitor information, one needs to ask what the morally significant difference is between pencil and paper and a dictating machine or an ear against the wall and the use of a glass, and second, that without fail business firms do not have clear signals on what to do with competitor information.

Both the moral significance of differences and the lack of clear signals require more comment. If lines are going to be drawn on individual activities that represent discrete choices under a category of activities, e.g. use of competitor information, it is important to define clearly what makes one activity permissible and another immoral. Indeed, in considering lists of activities such as that presented in *WHERE DO YOU DRAW THE LINE?*, when individual managers draw lines by saying no to certain activities, the explanation given for making choices is often in moral language, e.g. fairness or honesty.

The reality of the lack of clear signals is important to our discussion because it is precisely in those areas where the line between legal and illegal is not clear that it is essential that business firms define the limits of acceptable behavior for their employees. My experience in using the sample list of choices faced on the airplane and in the hotel is that within firms there is an amazing degree of lack of clarity on many similar issues.

To me, both the case presented above, JUST A LITTLE HELP, and the list of options on using competitor information, WHERE DO YOU DRAW THE LINE?, raise basic questions about the meaning of integrity. How and under what circumstances one uses information about competitor firms is a very ill-defined area. On the one hand, business espionage with advanced electronic technology is a growing enterprise and reverse engineering is a well-developed art in many high-tech industries. On the other hand, there are well published instances of major firms, such as IBM, returning a purloined bid or new product plans to a firm that has been victimized, along with the identity of the source of the information. The inconsistency within business concerning the use of competitor information, an inconsistency demonstrated in responses to our opening examples, provides a good basis for a closer examination of the meaning of ethics and business.

Many companies, including most of those that I have worked with, have corporate codes of ethics or credos. Invariably, words like fairness, honesty, and integrity figure prominently in the codes. But when I see the way that cases are analyzed and resolved — and the reasoning behind decisions — I question whether there is a clear, or appropriate, understanding of integrity and whether there is a clear understanding of what ethics is within business.

Webster's Dictionary, Third New International Edition, defines integrity in the following way: [2]

> 1. . . . an unimpaired or unmarred condition.
> 2. . . . . an uncompromising adherence to a code of moral, artistic or other values: utter sincerity, honesty, and candor: avoidance of deception, expediency, artificiality, or shallowness of any kind. (A review of the index to business periodicals for the three years from 1986 to 1989 in the Rice library, covering 810 periodicals, produced only *three* entries under "integrity.")

The definition of integrity, with its focus on "utter sincerity" and avoidance of "deception, expediency" etc. sets a high standard. Certainly when one looks at advertising, management-labor contract negotiations, announcement of new product lines never intended to be introduced and other accepted business practices, we are aware that integrity is understood in a quite different way than Webster would have it.

The proliferation of codes of ethics and corporate credos suggests that this is a good time not only to focus on the meaning of a word like integrity in business but on the larger topic of the meaning of ethics in business as well. We are in a climate today in which there is substantial focus on business ethics in colleges and universities, as well as in the media. There are also many programs and experiments within business focusing on ethics.

Knowledgeable people in firms, with or without ethics consultants, are working on new developments on how better to incorporate ethical considerations into all aspects of business. Certainly, change in this area, as in most areas of knowledge, will be incremental rather than characterized by the sudden discovery of the "silver bullet."

A clear understanding of how ethics is thought about in business and how it should be thought about may forward the development of the integration of ethics into business decisions and practices. It is to that subject that the remainder of this lecture is devoted as a way to bring all three lectures into a common focus.

ETHICS is used in differing ways and with differing understanding. For our purposes, we can define at least three ways—each of which relates to how ethics is understood and how ethics may be taught or integrated into a business setting.

Ethics as CHARACTER

Ethics as BEHAVIOR

Ethics as REFLECTION

First, *ethics as character*. The reference here is to a "good" or "bad" person. The common assertion here, often heard from managers in business ethics seminars, is that acting ethically is primarily a matter of an individual's character, which is formed and shaped by family, religious association, school, and community, probably immutably, long before the person joins a firm.

To a large extent, the above understanding of character formation is true; the individual's character certainly will not be changed in the brief exposure of a corporate ethics seminar or required reading of a corporate manual on business practices. Corporate ethics programs should not be aimed at changing the individual character.

Interestingly, though, one can undertake to define, reshape, or make explicit the corporate character of an organization. I take it that the efforts directed at defining a corporate credo are this type of activity. Similarly, various activities—such as executive seminars, videos featuring the CEO talking about corporate values, and repeated statement of the corporate credo in company publications—are designed to keep alive a self-conscious definition of corporate character.

These activities directed at developing or maintaining corporate character are familiar, and valuable, and will undoubtedly continue. We need to be clear, however, about what they do; they probably have little effect on changing an individual's moral character but they are valuable in providing reinforcement for a difficult moral choice and a warning to anyone tempted to engage in questionable or unsavory behavior.

Second, *ethics as behavior.* Another use of ethics is as an adjective in describing certain kinds of behavior. Every organization and profession has a set of guidelines and standards that defines good, or ethical, and bad, or non-ethical behavior. Doctors know that they *should* act for the well-being of the patient and should not do mercy killing. Public accountants know that they *should* retain their independence from their clients and should not obscure serious problems in their financial reports. Professors know that they *should* be thorough in their research and should not plagiarize. Law enforcement officers know that they *should* treat suspects fairly and should not take bribes. Ethical behavior is prescribed and proscribed in every profession and organization by tradition, by codes, and by manuals or policy statements.

Knowing what ethical behavior is is important and is something that organizations can and do do for themselves, and well. Much of the focus of activities under the rubric of corporate ethics programs falls into the category of defining and teaching what is expected and acceptable behavior. Codes of ethics; business conduct or business practice statements; seminars directed at defining fraud, waste, and abuse in government contracting, bribery, or unlawful use of insider information in commercial business are all efforts aimed at stating and communicating what is acceptable and unacceptable behavior.

In a presentation at the University of Southern California, the Chairman of General Dynamics described the program that had been developed and implemented for its employees. In sum, he said that past problems had resulted from a misunderstanding of the game that was being played. General Dynamics employees had been competing aggressively by the rules of football whereas the game was really basketball. The General Dynamics program, he went on, was not aimed at assessing blame for past behavior, rather it was designed to make it clear to its people what the game is and what its rules are.

In short, the General Dynamics program was described as rule *communication*. Another General Dynamics representative described similar goals and said something to the effect that "our program is not designed to make philosophers or ethicists out of our managers." Instead, it provides clear guidelines.

Rule oriented programs, codes, and statements are essential to any organization. Although that work is never fully done, I think that business firms have learned to do that well.

Third, *ethics as reflection*. A third way of using ethics in the business setting is that of ethical reflection geared (1) toward resolving ethical dilemmas in particular situations or cases and (2) toward normative analysis directed at defining company norms and standards, as well as subsequent policy.

It is on this third way of looking at ethics that I want to focus in this lecture. I will deal with ethical reflection by addressing in turn the *what*, the *how*, and the *why*.

First, the *what*, that is the topics and concerns that need to be addressed more thoroughly. I think that it is critical to focus on basic norms and principles, such as integrity, honesty, fairness, and justice and to consider their meaning and application to a firm and its business. I have chosen integrity as my focus because it is so common in company codes and credos and business practice statements.

Consider the cases that we have examined in these lectures. In *Resort Properties*, where Joe Straightshooter faced the question about disclosing a potential flooding problem, does withholding, though lawful, meet the Webster's definition of sincerity, honesty, and candor?

In the dial-a-porn case, does the failure of the companies to pursue legal initiatives to terminate the adult message service, by falling back on the law, meet the test of sincerity? This question is especially pointed in the light of the many statements about the repugnance the companies had for the dial-a-porn messages. In *Resort Properties*, Joe and ICI could argue that the law did not require reporting the flood problem. In the dial-a-porn case, company representatives asserted that the law prohibited them from actions directed toward terminating the porn services.

I emphasize these responses because I so often see this falling back on the law as defining the limits of any response and being equated with ethical behavior. A phrase I like to use about this kind of response is "going to the specs." A case from a defense industry company that I use involves the question of whether or not to disclose a serious, but cosmetic, defect in an aircraft. The project is over budget, behind schedule, and repairing the flaw, which might not be discovered immediately, or at all, will take 700 person hours. The first question (and often the decisive one for the discussion) is always, "Is it in the specs?" The "specs" represent another from of law that defines behavior.

JUST A LITTLE HELP and WHERE DO YOU DRAW THE LINE?, the situations with which we introduced this lecture, pose at their core integrity questions in relation to honesty and deception. It is important to bear in mind that these cases have been written by managers participating in programs within companies with whom I have been working which all have strong integrity statements.

What the treatment of the cases illustrate to me, through a great deal of experience with them with corporate groups, is (1) the tendency to look for resolution in legal requirements and operational terms (what are the Specs), and (2) uncertainty or disagreement over the meaning of norms, like integrity, when applied to the operational setting, and division over the nature and self- identity of the organization.

Second, the *how*, suggests ways to build on programs already in place to prepare managers to deal with ethical reflection more adequately. Each of the following suggestions will require commitment and time on the part of both firms and managers.

1. Provide support for several managers to take course work in ethics and business ethics, as part of an MBA or as stand alone courses.

For many firms, this would fit a normal kind of educational support and advancement program, and thus would not require any departure from standard practice.

2. Support one or more managers through a Master's degree in ethics, with a focus on business ethics.

This would obviously be expensive and time consuming, but would be like support for an MBA, a common practice, but with a different focus. This kind of program is especially appropriate for business managers assigned to head up ethics programs within firms. I have encountered a substantial number of such managers who have been in the legal department or human resources for many years before taking on the ethics assignment. In many cases, these managers have reported that they have no formal ethics background.

The suggestion of a Master's program is based on a model that comes from my experience with medical ethics. I teach a course for senior pre-meds at the USC medical school in which small groups of students are taken by physicians to see patients with whom they are dealing—AIDS patients, very young premature babies with complications, comatose patients in the intensive care ward, badly burned patients, etc.

The physicians approach the pre-meds as they do medical students; that is, they take students who are highly academically trained and qualified and they confront them with the history, diagnosis, and prognosis for a particular patient at the bedside. They describe the situation, e. g. this patient has a one in fifteen chance of surviving even with major surgery, and the parents are coming to talk to me tomorrow. They then ask the students what they would say.

The point is that the students are academically trained, but they need the application. But that is not the end of the story.

The head of the burn ward, highly trained and experienced, recognized that the medical decisions he faced—to perform surgery, not to perform surgery; to do skin grafts, not to do skin grafts; to insert a respirator and a nasal feeding tube, or not—were in his competency. However, questions about whether the patient or parents can refuse treatment even if death would follow, or who should make that decision, were moral or ethical choices.

The burn ward physician, skilled as he was in medicine, was not prepared to deal fully with those questions for himself and for his burn ward team.

Accordingly, he pursued a Master's in social ethics over a two year period while continuing his work. After the degree program he was better prepared to make his own decisions, but he was also able to give much more guidance to his whole team.

The point is that this is a reversal of the student model; the practitioner needed the academic background to address the ethical issues. An illustration that is closer to business is the senior partner in a big-eight accounting firm who is presently taking a Ph.D. in social ethics while continuing his practice.

3. Based on suggestions 1 and 2 above, develop a cadre of ethics experts within the firm.

One possibility for this would be to form an ethics reflection group or committee. The committee would be assigned the task of providing guidance on specific sticky issues. It would also be asked to think beyond the immediate situation and its resolution to the basic issues that are raised as a way to reflect on policy.

Even better, a firm could follow the lead of many hospitals with ethics committees established to respond to difficult issues that a physician or health care team raises and have one or more trained ethicists external to the company on the committee. These experts can provide the background and perspective to go with the operational and technical knowledge that managers possess.

4. The medical school course for pre-meds also suggests a pattern that could be used for senior business majors. Intern programs are common in business, only this would be a program focused on ethical dilemmas in various industries and disciplines.

5. Form an industry-wide or trans-company standing committee or task force to reflect on generic issues as they arise.

A model here would be the peer review committees in medical centers, called Institutional Review Boards, which assess proposed experiments with human subjects with an eye to evaluating whether the proposed procedures pass ethical muster.

6. As an adjunct, or perhaps prior to, any of the suggestions above, it is crucial to insure that there are incentives through the reward system to encourage the exercise of integrity.

Recall studies of affirmative action programs. The Chairman of a firm would send out a directive that affirmative action was to be taken seriously, admonishing all division heads to meet target goals. Nothing would happen. The directive from the Chairman would be repeated. Still nothing would happen. Why? Because the performance review and bonus plan was based wholly on meeting production targets, with no reward or penalty attached to meeting or failing to meet affirmative action goals.

When the system was changed in some firms so that a portion of the annual assessment was tied to meeting affirmative action goals, things began to change.

The same kind of attention to assessment of performance against integrity standards needs to be built into the reward system. At present, there is some punishment for wrong doing (depending on whether it becomes public and whether a contract was won or lost), but there is very little reward for right doing. Granted, one is expected to do one's job well, but in sit-

uations of extreme pressure—and extreme tempta-
tion—some reward for sticking one's neck out on behalf
of maintaining the firm's integrity and preventing a
harm, even at the loss of immediate business, needs to
be in place.

Third, the *why*. Why should business firms think
about engaging in programs designed to enhance ethical
reflection as a basis for doing that which is beyond legal
requirements?

This is somewhat harder to sell to business firms,
especially without sounding like a sermonic appeal to be
good citizens. There are several important reasons,
though, including:

• prevention, or self-interest.

Indeed, this may be the strongest motivating force
for the increase in ethics programs and a sound reason
for taking such efforts seriously. Firms should have
good reason to avoid such situations as Ford with its
Pinto or A. H. Robins with its Dalkon shield.

• self-understanding of what the firm is or wants to
become—the definition of corporate culture and values.

This is where the third emphasis, on ethics as
reflection, plays back in a loop on ethics as character.

• to take the oft-stated objective to be a good corporate citizen a step further.

An example comes from the savings and loan
industry. When a major savings and loan organization
in Detroit was faced with protests over alleged red-lining, it cited its fiduciary duty to its stockholders and
depositors and stone-walled, refusing to change or to
meet with community leaders. This behavior changed

when protests and picketing, and threats of massive deposit withdrawals, necessitated a different response.

In contrast, when a leading savings and loan institution in Pittsburgh was faced with the same challenge over alleged red-lining, it took the initiative to galvanize business, banking, government and community groups to restore the inner city.

The Detroit S and L was working within the law; the Pittsburgh S and L went beyond the legal requirements, at some expense and risk on its own, to be a good corporate citizen.

• to build a stronger case for self-governance.

Self-governance requires accountability and industry-wide committees would go some way to doing what professions do in setting their own standards.

• finally, the familiar "good ethics is good business."

There is growing evidence that the oft-stated phrase about good ethics and good business is in fact true. To an extent, this is another version of self-interest, with a focus on the impact on the bottom line. It obviously makes sense, since attending to the best interests of customers, employees, communities, and stockholders will finally serve to enhance business. It does need to be noted that there may be some short run risks or costs.

Conclusion

In all three of these lectures, we have dealt with situations drawn from actual business experience in which firms and managers have been faced with ethical dilemmas. In each case, the response of the firms involved was to look to the law for ethical guidelines. It is my contention that such an appeal to the law is not adequate if a firm wants to take ethics seriously. Thus the argument for enhancing ethics programs and ethics preparation so that the dimension of reflection is added to corporate efforts.

In *Resort Properties*, non-disclosure, though legal, would put a customer, and possible future condominium purchasers, at risk. In the *Dial-a-Porn* case, by acting solely on the basis of legal remedies, the telephone companies risked psychological (and possibly physical) injury to minors as well as damage to their own reputations. In JUST A LITTLE HELP, the firm that used the competitor's bid, acting on shaky, but possibly, legal grounds, lost not only the contract in the case but suffered serious injury to its reputation and chances for future business with the major customer. In WHERE DO YOU DRAW THE LINE?, a number of legal activities, if pursued, would certainly have violated any common understanding of integrity and put company reputations at risk.

Essentially, then, the situations described in the three lectures reveal a limited vision of ethics within business firms which tends to plateau at the level of the law and demonstrate the need for an expanded understanding of ethics that includes reflection. That the cases used and situations described are real situations represents the all too common status of ethics in business firms today. That a number of firms are beginning and expanding ethics programs indicates that there are opportunities for achieving the needed expanded understanding of ethics in business and integration of ethics into business decision-making and practices.

Notes

1. Goldman, Alan, "Business Ethics: Profits, Utilities, and Moral Rights," *Philosophy and Public Affairs*, 9 No. 3, p. 261.

2. G & C Merriam Co, Springfield, Mass, 1961.